While

Mrs. Coverlet

Was

Away

With Drawings by **GARRETT PRICE**

While

Mrs. Coverlet

Was

Away

by Mary Nash

LITTLE, BROWN AND COMPANY

Boston, Toronto

Published simultaneously in Canada
by Little, Brown & Company (Canada) Limited

PRINTED IN THE UNITED STATES OF AMERICA

While

Mrs. Coverlet

Was

Away

Chapter I

THE three Persever children were eating supper in the kitchen: Malcolm the oldest, Molly the middle one, and the Toad (his name was really Theobold), who was only six. At the table with them sat Mrs. Coverlet, their stout housekeeper. She had a pile of white hair and a busy red face. Next to her daughter Marygold in Duluth, and Marygold's husband John, and Marygold's twin babies, she loved the Persever family better than anybody. Mrs. Coverlet was cutting a chocolate pie into four pieces — an enormous slice for Malcolm, two ordinary-sized pieces for Molly and the Toad, and a sliver no thicker than a leaf for herself.

"I hope you're not on a diet again, Mrs. Coverlet!" Molly declared. "It's so hard on your disposition." Molly, as usual, was speaking the simple truth, but as she had so often noticed before, the person she was speaking it to did not seem a bit glad to hear it.

Instead, Mrs. Coverlet frowned, turned to Malcolm, and handed him his dessert. "If we could have a little quiet here," she remarked, "I'm sure I'd like to hear Malcolm read your dear father's letter from New Zealand."

Under ordinary circumstances the Persevers' father was not in New Zealand, but right there with them in Loganbury. He was a vitamin salesman, the best one they had at Bouncer's Drug Company. Mr. Bouncer said that Mr. Persever was a living testimonial to the wonderful effects of Vitabounce, his product. Certainly, nobody who felt puny or tired could resist Mr. Persever's snapping eyes and powerful handshake. Naturally, all the Persever children

and Mrs. Coverlet ate Bouncer's Vitabounce, and they, too, were full of high spirits and energy. The floor of the hall closet in the Persevers' house was always stacked with samples of Vitabounce so that Mr. Persever could offer a capsule or two to guests who looked seedy or down at the mouth.

One day a few weeks ago, Mr. Persever had received an astonishing letter from a lawyer in Wellington, New Zealand. It explained that an old bachelor named Jetsom Persever had died there, leaving as his only property an abandoned tin mine. Thorough search had shown that the American Persevers were Jetsom's only living relatives. The lawyer's letter went on to suggest that since Mr. Persever lived so far from the mine, which was not operating anyway, he ought to try to sell it. Instead, the children's father decided to go to New Zealand and see the mine for himself. "The opportunity of a lifetime!" the energetic man had exclaimed, and then he had hurried down to Mr. Bouncer's office to arrange for a month off.

Dear Children and Mrs. Coverlet [began the letter from New Zealand which Malcolm was now reading aloud],

How is everybody managing? I'm camping out in one of the old buildings at the mine, and I'm positive I can get it operating again. The only thing I wish I had is more money for equipment and repairs. You know, without my salary from Bouncer's Drug Company, things are bound to be a

little tight for all of us. You can help a lot there at home by pulling in your belts until I get this mine going. Not that I want anybody to worry. Everything is going well here, and I'm staying on this job till it's done. Go to Mr. Vault at the bank when you need funds. I left money there for you. If there's anything troubling anybody, see Reverend Forthright about it. And remember that Miss Eva Penalty offered to take the Toad at her house, if Mrs. Coverlet should need a rest or time off.

Love to all,
Dad

"*Won't* go to Miss Eva's! Ever, ever, *ever!*" announced the small but fierce Toad, beetling his brow down over his brown eyes. "I'll lock myself in the bathroom and squirt her with my water pistol through the keyhole if she tries to come get me!"

"Hush now," Mrs. Coverlet murmured calmly, helping herself to a second skinny morsel of pie, no thicker than a piece of tracing paper. "You don't have to go to Miss Eva's — though she's a lovely soul, and *so* fond of you."

At Mrs. Coverlet's words Malcolm and Molly looked curiously at their brother. They could never understand what an old maid like Miss Eva Penalty could see in such a tough and grimy boy. Naturally, *they* were rather fond of him and, ever since their mother died, when he was still a baby, had been doing their best to raise and civilize him (with the occasional help of Mrs. Coverlet and their father).

"Do you want me to read to you before bed, Toad?" asked his sister Molly. She had taken on the chore of improving her little brother's mind, but it was certainly slow work.

"Yup," he replied, noisily scraping his pie plate before he jumped up from the table. "I want *Snow White and Roast Beef.*"

"*Rose Red,*" Molly corrected him firmly as she and the Toad left the kitchen to find the storybook.

Malcolm and Mrs. Coverlet remained sitting at the kitchen table. Mrs. Coverlet looked worried as she absent-mindedly helped herself to a third slice of chocolate pie, no thicker than a wisp of cobweb. "Will we get along all right?" she suddenly asked Malcolm. She asked his advice a good bit, now that he was thirteen. "Has your father much money for us there in Mr. Vault's bank? Will it last us, do you think? He's *such* a ways off in New Zealand!"

"Don't worry, Mrs. Coverlet," replied Malcolm in a manly voice. He gave her a wise and confident smile. "If our money gets low, we'll have to make some ourselves, that's all."

Mrs. Coverlet smiled back at him, but not very broadly. And I'm not sure that Malcolm had entirely relieved her mind.

Chapter II

A WEEK or so later, on a Saturday morning in June, the three Persevers were in Malcolm's room making up their minds what to do that day. Malcolm was lying across his bed with his hands under his head and his feet in their work boots propped against the wall. Industrious Molly sat cross-legged on the floor polishing her saddle shoes. You could not see the Toad, for he was under the bed with Nervous, his tortoise-shell cat, and nothing showed of their private game but an occasional flash of orange tail, and a slight twitching of the skirt of the bedspread.

"Malcolm! Take your feet off the wall!" Molly exclaimed, as she looked up from her work to blow on a shoe. "Look at that horrible scratch you've already made!"

When Malcolm lifted his boots and saw the scarred wallpaper beneath them, he groaned. "Well, I have to put them some place, don't I?" he asked bitterly. "I gave Mrs.

10

Coverlet my sacred word I wouldn't put my boots on the spread again." Here the poor boy raised his long legs straight in the air and stared sadly at the heavy boots. "Reverend Forthright says I have one of the most complicated consciences he's ever run across," he remarked, with a sort of gloomy pride. "He says it may be years before I adjust to it."

"My goodness, Malcolm! Why don't you just take your boots off?" asked practical Molly.

Just then the Toad's muffled voice inquired, "What did we decide to do today?"

"The first thing *I* have to do is mow Miss Eva's grass," Malcolm replied, sitting up and carefully spreading out a piece of Kleenex on the edge of the bedside table and lowering his heels onto it to rest. There was not much room for feet on that small wobbly table, which Malcolm had made in school the year before. A lamp stood there already, to say nothing of a pyramid of books, two partly finished airplane models, and several water-color sets. "I gave Miss Eva my sacred word I'd cut her grass Saturday before I did another thing."

"Why don't you go do it, then?" Molly asked, as she brushed her yellow hair back out of her eyes and watched her older brother stretch out comfortably on the bed again.

"If you two came and helped me rake and trim, I'd

finish a lot sooner, and then we could all go turtle hunting in the slough."

"Good! Let's go!" The feet and legs of the eager Toad began to emerge from under Malcolm's bed.

But at once his sister said, "Get back under, Toad! I don't see why we should always have to help Malcolm when he's the only one she pays." The legs and feet were obligingly drawn in. "All Miss Eva does when we go over there is stick her head out of the window and say aren't we sweet little children to help our big brother, and please don't tramp in her flowers."

Now they heard a gruff voice singing to itself under the bed, "I *hate* you, dear Miss *Ee*-va. I rih-hi-hilly *do*-oo."

"Cut that out, Toad!" snapped Malcolm, horrified at the song. He twisted sideways, hung his head and shoulders over the edge of the bed, and lifted the spread so the Toad could get the full benefit of his older brother's red, upside-down frown. The little table where Malcolm's feet were now pressing with all his weight gave an exhausted croak. "*Never* say things like that about people!" continued the boy with the complicated conscience. "What if we *do* think she's an old — I mean — you'd feel pretty bad if her house burned down or something after what you've said!"

"Oh, ye-ah?" was the Toad's shocking reply. But no-

13

body had time to notice it, for at that moment one leg of the table bent inward under Malcolm's weight, and the whole thing began to collapse with a slow, ripping sound, accompanied by many small thuds and clanks as everything on it slid to the floor. At these interesting noises, the Toad popped his head out from beneath the bed, just as the table itself crashed over. Nervous, his orange and black cat, made one of her most spectacular leaps from beneath the spread, straight through the air, and out the open window to the porch roof beyond. Malcolm, looking down from the bed at the top of the Toad's brown head, saw a thin red stream begin to trickle in front of both ears.

"Quick, Molly!" he gasped. "The table fell on the Toad and his head's split wide open!"

"Really?" demanded the Toad in great excitement. "Come look inside, Molly, and see if I have many brains in there, and what attaches my eyes in the back!"

"Don't be silly!" his sister told him as she came and bent down to see. "That red stuff is only paint water. You're not even scratched! Now come out from under there and wash off your face!"

"Bossy!" muttered her ungrateful little brother. "You always ruin everything! Malcolm said it was *so* cut open!" He retired behind the bedspread, still stubbornly feeling his head for the split.

What with sponging up the paint water, collecting the

damp books, and reasoning with each other about whose water-color pads were the two which were totally soaked and spoiled, and whose was the one which was miraculously dry, the Persevers scarcely noticed when the phone rang downstairs and Mrs. Coverlet answered it.

Then all of a sudden their housekeeper was standing in Malcolm's doorway, flustered and panting. "What's a body to do? What's a body to do?" she gasped, sitting down on the edge of Malcolm's bed and wiping her face with a corner of her apron. The children dropped their mopping operations and came and stood beside her sympathetically. And they began to realize that something must be very wrong indeed when Mrs. Coverlet not only did not notice the wreckage on the bedroom floor but was too distracted even to see that the Toad's face was wildly streaked, like an Indian's, with red paint water.

Chapter III

"WHAT'S the matter, Mrs. Coverlet?" Malcolm asked their housekeeper in a gentle voice.

"Marygold!" poor Mrs. Coverlet was able at last to blurt. "Fallen and broken her leg! That was John-me-son-in-law on the phone from Duluth!"

"Heavens, Mrs. Coverlet!" Molly exclaimed. "Who's looking after the twin babies?"

"Who indeed! Who indeed!" moaned Mrs. Coverlet, rocking back and forth on the edge of Malcolm's bed. "The darlings — not six weeks old! And John, their father, working nights and days and overtime at the plant!"

"You'll have to go to Duluth right away," Malcolm said firmly.

"And leave yourselves? Poor fatherless babes that you are!" Mrs. Coverlet burst into tears at the very suggestion.

"Nonsense, Mrs. Coverlet," Molly reassured her, patting her shoulder. "It won't be for long. Just till Marygold can get around."

"Why, you know us!" added Malcolm cheerfully. "We can manage!"

"Theobold could always go to Miss Eva's," Mrs. Coverlet reflected, drying her eyes. At this prospect the Toad lowered his brows and turned a really hideous shade of plum behind the red paint. "And the Reverend Forthright could sleep up here at night in your father's room so you two big ones wouldn't be alone."

"I'll get the timetable. There's one in Dad's desk," sensible Molly offered, and she bustled out of the room.

"Oh, but who'll tidy the house — and cook — and weed — and — and air the beds — prune the roses — empty the garbage!" sobbed Mrs. Coverlet, going to pieces again as she named just a few of the things that surely would go to ruin if she left.

"Don't worry," Malcolm consoled her. "We'll take care of everything. We won't disgrace you."

"Only one train to Duluth today. That's at noon," Molly announced, coming into the room with the timetable. "You can make it if we hurry. Malcolm, call a cab!" And although Mrs. Coverlet protested and changed her mind a dozen times right up to the moment the cab honked outside, she did pack a few things, put on her good hat, and let herself be escorted down the front walk by Molly and Malcolm.

"Where's Theobold?" asked Mrs. Coverlet after they had helped her into the back seat of the taxi and she was leaning forward to hug them good-by. "Saints preserve me! In all the rush I've not spoke to Miss Eva about him, nor to the Reverend about you two! Here, help me out!" She held out both plump arms to them, but sensible Molly closed the door firmly and politely.

"There really isn't time, Mrs. Coverlet," she said, poking her yellow head through the open taxi window. "You've barely got twenty minutes to make it as it is. Don't worry, now! We'll see them both today." And with that, Mrs. Coverlet was driven away, her red, worried face keeping them in sight from the window as long as she could.

When Malcolm and Molly came back indoors, the house had a breathless, shaken look. The timetable was lying on the hall floor; there was a damp dish towel on the telephone stand which Mrs. Coverlet had forgotten there after her phone call from Duluth. The coat closet was open, and on the floor inside they could see the tumbled stacks of Mr. Persever's vitamin samples, where the Toad had been rooting about helpfully for Mrs. Coverlet's lost umbrella.

"By the way, where *is* the Toad?" asked Molly uneasily.

"Toad!" Malcolm called, and though there was no answer, they presently heard a faint "Me-a-ow" from upstairs, followed by a scuffle and a cross whisper which said, "Qui-et, Nervous!"

"He's in the bathroom with his cat!" Molly exclaimed. "And I'll bet he's locked the door like he said he would if he had to go to Miss Eva's!"

"Come on out, Toad," Malcolm called kindly. "You can't stay there!"

miss Eva

"I'm *not* going to Miss Eva's!" snarled the Toad's voice through the bathroom keyhole.

"You'll get awful hungry in there," his practical sister warned him.

"Ha! That's what you think! I brought up three loaves of bread and a big jar of peanut butter, and I'm never coming out!"

Molly was starting up the front stairs to reason with the foolish child when Malcolm took her arm. "Wait a sec," he advised, and they sat down side by side on the bottom step. "Exactly what did you say to Mrs. Coverlet about us speaking to Miss Eva and Mr. Forthright today?"

Molly looked puzzled. "Why, you heard, Malcolm. Mrs.

Coverlet said she'd forgotten to tell them she was going, and about looking after us, and I said she didn't have time, but not to worry, we'd see them today."

"Good!" Malcolm nodded in relief. "We can see them today, all right, since you gave her your word. We usually do see them every day, since they both live so close. But you didn't say we'd see them today and tell them that Mrs. Coverlet's gone to Duluth, did you?"

"No-o-o," Molly replied. "But I don't see — I mean, that's what Mrs. Coverlet thought I meant, so —"

"Listen, Molly, suppose nobody knew we were here alone! Then the Toad wouldn't need to go to Miss Eva's, and Mr. Forthright wouldn't have to sleep up here. We could go on just the way we are — in peace and quiet."

"Why, Malcolm!" cried the astonished Molly. "What about your conscience? Are we supposed to lie?"

"Lie!" The boy with the complicated conscience shuddered. "Of course not! If somebody comes right out and asks us, 'Where's Mrs. Coverlet?' we'll have to say, 'In Duluth.' But if we just don't happen to mention it, maybe nobody will ask. How would anybody know?"

Molly considered the whole extraordinary idea for several moments. It did seem a shame to send the poor Toad to Miss Eva's, where he was bound to be miserable, as well as infuriated — she was sure to scrub his ears and change his clothes and give him many more boiled vegetables than

were necessary. Besides, fond as Malcolm and she were of Reverend Forthright, it would be much more — well, relaxing — to stay here by themselves. And after all, she thought, if Malcolm's delicate conscience felt this was the right thing to do, it certainly needn't bother *her* practical mind.

"How long do you suppose Mrs. Coverlet'll be gone?" she asked finally.

"Oh, a few days — maybe a week," replied Malcolm with comfortable vagueness.

"O.K. Let's do it!" she agreed. "Now we'd better go up and tell the Toad right away, before he makes himself sick on peanut butter. I could hear him rustling the bread wrappings the whole time we've been sitting here."

"Watch out!" roared the Toad with his mouth full, as he heard their approaching steps outside the door. "I've got my water pistol loaded!"

"Open up!" said his older brother patiently as a jet of water hissed past his ear. "We've decided you don't have to go to Miss Eva's. No, really, Toad, I'm not fooling! Sacred word! Hey, stop that, Toad!"

24

Chapter IV

HERE comes the Toad up the outside cellar steps, look-ing to right and to left to see if Malcolm or Molly is watching. Although it is the middle of June — a week

since Mrs. Coverlet left — the day is windy, and the sun slips undecidedly in and out. And yet the Toad has nothing on but his old blue bathing suit; nothing, that is, but his bathing suit and a coil of garden hose draped around his neck. At the top of the steps he lifts this off and attaches one end to a faucet by the side of the house. Then he pulls the length of hose, a brass sprinkler at the end, out into the middle of the back yard. He runs back and turns on the faucet, and here comes the water! The Toad holds out one bare leg into the spray. Its five toes wriggle furiously, and turn a frozen blue. The Toad pulls back his leg and frowns thoughtfully down at his blue toes. Now he is turning away from the sprinkler and going down the cellar steps again. Thank goodness he has given up his plan on such a chilly day! But what is this coming up the steps now? Apparently it is a huge orange bug with a small brown head, walking on two enormously thick black legs. Oh, no, it is only the Toad again, wearing an adult-size orange life jacket and his father's black rubber fishing boots.

When Molly caught sight of her little brother running back and forth through the lawn sprinkler in this curious costume, she leaned her head out of her bedroom window and called, "*Theo*bold Persever! On a cold day like this!"

The Toad did not look up. He was in the middle of a daring leap right over the brass sprinkler itself. But when he

was out of the spray, he called to her, "Not cold, Molly!
Vivvr-vivvr-life jacket — vrr — boots — keep me vivver-
vivver warm!"

"Get out of that water and come inside this instant!"
was his sister's only reply. She was waiting for him at the
front door with a towel over her arm. "Don't drip in the
hall!" she scolded. "Take your boots off right there on
the porch! Then go straight upstairs to the bathroom and
I'll help you!"

"Bu-bub-bub-bossy!" muttered the Toad between chat-
tering teeth as he started up the front stairs ahead of her.

Molly knelt on the bathroom floor beside him and
worked at the knots of wet tape which held the orange life

27

jacket together. "You know it's no day for playing in the sprinkler," she said. "Hold still!" He was wriggling and shivering in the most exasperating way. "Now that there are no grownups around to watch us, Toad, you've got to learn to think! Children on their own have to use their brains!"

At these last words the Toad stopped shivering. His eyes narrowed, and his small chest inside the sopping jacket swelled with importance. He even forgot to say, "Bossy!" — which he always did at the end of Molly's lectures. He was too busy regarding himself in the bathroom mirror and trying to look like a child-on-its-own who has lots of brains and constantly uses them.

"There!" Molly said as the last strap came free and the jacket slid off. "I'll put it here in the tub to drip. Now if you hurry and get dressed, I'll have time to read to you before we fix supper."

"Want to hear 'Repulsive, Repulsive, let down your hair,' " ordered the Toad, pulling his T shirt over his head.

Naturally, Molly opened her mouth to correct him. "Rapunzel, Rapunzel" was on the tip of her tongue, to be said in her most big-sisterly voice. But all at once, looking at the small Toad squirming into his clothes, clumsily as usual, but as fast as he could, she thought to herself what a cheerful and unwhining little boy he was — all things considered. And it occurred to her that it must be rather

28

hard, at six, to be an entirely reasonable person, simple as it was when you were ten, like herself. And so, just this once, she gave up the pleasure of correcting her little brother and helped him thread his belt through the loops in the back of his trousers instead. Then they went downstairs together, squeezed side by side into the big chair in the living room, and opened the storybook across their laps.

At this moment, down the street, Malcolm was stretched out on the couch in Reverend Forthright's living room. His feet in their scuffed work boots lay upon the cushions at one end, like a couple of sleeping puppies. Malcolm was always able to make himself very comfortable at his friend's, because Mr. Forthright was a bachelor and had no one, not even a housekeeper, to explain to him about the horror of shoes on the furniture. Apparently no one had ever told him that you must serve cake on plates when you eat it in the living room, either, for both he and Malcolm were holding large, black, crumbly slices of devil's food in their bare hands. Now, the ladies in Mr. Forthright's church felt so sad to think of their minister struggling to look after himself in his little house that when they were not urging him to their homes "for at least one solid meal," they were baking things for him and then stopping around secretly to slip the dishes inside the screen door of his back porch. I believe no one in Loganbury had a more rich and varied diet than Mr. Forthright.

"Wonderful cake of Miss Eva's, isn't it?" remarked Mr. Forthright.

"Thought you didn't know who made it," Malcolm said, licking his fingers.

"That was before I tasted it. Miss Eva always puts a dash of almond flavor in her icing. Trade mark, you might say." After a while Mr. Forthright asked Malcolm how his conscience had been behaving lately. Being a special friend of Malcolm's, and knowing how much trouble it gave him, he never failed to inquire about it sympathetically.

"Uh — pretty good, sir," Malcolm answered, hesitating for only a second as he thought about Mrs. Coverlet. But his complicated conscience told him clearly that his first duty lay in saving his younger brother from going to Miss Eva's in any way he could manage it — short of actually lying, of course.

The minister was glad to hear that Malcolm's conscience was giving him no discomfort these days. "Wouldn't be surprised if you learned to live quite comfortably with it in time," he said.

"I sure hope so!" Malcolm answered, with feeling.

"Any news about when your father is getting back?"

"We had another letter Thursday," Malcolm told him. "He says there's a lot of work to getting a mine going, but as long as we're O.K., he wants to stay there and see it through."

"Naturally," Mr. Forthright agreed. But he was frowning a little as he got up, thrust his hands in the pockets of his old gray sweater, and went over to the window. "There's something I've got to talk to you about, Malcolm," he said, looking out at his yard between the curtains. "That's why I asked you over."

Malcolm, who had just taken an especially big bite of cake, stopped chewing, and his cheeks and eyes bulged with alarm. He was wondering if his friend suspected anything about Mrs. Coverlet, and if he would be able to reassure him while still staying strictly honest.

"I had a phone call from your father's friend Mr. Vault, at the bank," explained Mr. Forthright, coming back and taking his old seat. "He says there's very little left in your father's account, and he wonders if we ought to write him." At these words, which showed that Mr. Forthright was not going to ask any difficult questions about Mrs. Coverlet, Malcolm let out his breath in a gusty sigh of relief.

"I know, I know that's bad news," said the minister sympathetically, thinking Malcolm's sigh was caused by his anxiety over their financial situation. "And in view of what you tell me about your father's plans to stay on longer in New Zealand, I'm afraid we will have to let him know that the family will soon need more funds."

"Oh, gosh, Mr. Forthright!" Malcolm exclaimed, now listening in alarm to what his friend was saying. "If you write him about it, he'll probably leave the mine and come right home. The mine hasn't made any money yet, so he can't send us any from New Zealand. Why, it would be awful to make him give up his mine when he's worked so hard!"

Mr. Forthright nodded his head sadly.

"I'm sure we can manage!" Malcolm insisted. By now his sensitive conscience was pricking him sharply at the idea of his father's having to give up his New Zealand adventure and come back home to earn money for three able-bodied children with nothing to do all summer vacation but amuse themselves. In his mind he was wildly casting about for some way to prevent Mr. Forthright's writing to his father. Yet he could think of no way in the world to do it. Malcolm sat up on the couch, put his feet on the floor, and, leaning forward, buried his head in his hands. "I wish you wouldn't let Dad know about it, Mr. Forthright," he said with real despair in his voice. "I know we could earn enough money ourselves!"

Mr. Forthright look sympathetically at his young friend. He was thinking to himself that though he had always believed he understood Malcolm, the boy was even more proud and sensitive, and his conscience even more complicated, than he had realized. "A letter must be written,

old fellow," he said gently. Malcolm did not look up. "Would this help?" asked Mr. Forthright. "Would you rather write him yourself? Do you want Mr. Vault and me to keep our noses out of it?"

At this, Malcolm's heart gave a sudden, sly thud. There *might* be a chance to save the situation after all! "Well —" he said slowly. "I *was* thinking of writing Dad tonight."

"Fine, then!" said the minister. "But no putting it off, Malcolm! I want your promise you'll get it into the mail tonight!"

"Sure, Mr. Forthright! Sacred word!" Malcolm hastily got up and made for the front door. "Good-by, Mr. Forthright!" he called cheerfully over his shoulder as he started out. "Thanks for the cake and all!"

Unfortunately, Mr. Forthright had followed him and looked after him in a puzzled way as Malcolm bounded down the porch steps. "Malcolm!" he called. Malcolm held his breath and turned around. "Your sudden eagerness to write this letter bothers me a little," said Mr. Forthright thoughtfully. "Remember, I've had considerable experience with your complicated conscience. Your fingers don't happen to be crossed all this time, by any chance?" But Malcolm obligingly held up both hands and wriggled all ten fingers separately.

When he came through the back door into the kitchen, he found Molly and the Toad getting supper. "Is that

butter you're using?" he demanded in a shocked voice as Molly dropped a large square of it into the frying pan.

"You can see it is, Malcolm," his sister answered dryly.

"Well, use bacon fat from now on," advised the noble boy, folding his arms and frowning disapprovingly at the spreading golden glob. "It's lots cheaper."

"What's eating you tonight, Malcolm?" Molly inquired, looking at Malcolm with her annoyingly keen gaze.

"There's to be a conference at supper," Malcolm announced mysteriously. "I'll explain to you then."

"Good! What about?" asked the Toad, who was setting the kitchen table in the corner. Oh, how he hoped it would be an opportunity to practice using his brains! He knew very well that *his* brains had never had much exercise; and now that he was a child-on-its-own he was anxious to develop them at every opportunity.

"It's to be about ways of making money," answered his older brother solemnly. And just as Malcolm might have expected, Molly immediately opened her mouth to ask a practical question. But he was in no mood for practical questions. He had been fending them off at Reverend Forthright's already. And so he put out his arm and pushed open the swinging door that led into the dining room. "We'll talk later," he told them loftily. "I've got to write Dad now. Gave Mr. Forthright my sacred word I'd do it tonight."

And Malcolm did exactly what he had promised. He wrote his father an interesting letter telling about the last week of school, about everybody's report cards (which were not bad), about how well the family was managing, and how the Toad was still waiting patiently from day to day for Nervous to have kittens. But he never said a word about Mrs. Coverlet's sudden trip to Duluth, or their needing money, because, although he had promised Mr. Forthright he would write his father, he had *never* mentioned what he was going to say. And when he was finished, Malcolm stamped the letter and ran down to the corner to mail it before Molly called him to supper. Because if he had put it off, his complicated conscience would have bothered him, and he couldn't have enjoyed a bite.

Chapter V

"WE have nearly used up the money Dad left in the bank for us!" Malcolm dramatically informed his younger brother and sister as he took his place across from them at the supper table.

"Better write Dad about it right away, then," suggested Molly with her usual matter-of-factness, "or is that what you were doing before supper?"

"We are *not* going to tell Dad a thing about it!" her brother bellowed at her.

"But —"

"It is a question of principle!" Malcolm thundered. And at this Molly shrugged and closed her mouth, for whenever she saw that Malcolm's conscience was involved in something, she knew from long experience that there was no use reasoning with him.

"Suppose we did tell Dad—what would happen?" Malcolm demanded, frowning sternly at his brother and sister like an arithmetic teacher with a question the class ought to know but doesn't. *"I'll* tell you what he'd do!" he told them, when all they did was stare at him stupidly. "He'd jump on a plane and leave his mine and go back to work at Mr. Bouncer's. How would you feel if he did that, while we sat here perfectly able-bodied, not lifting a finger! And in the summertime! When we don't even have school!"

Molly and the Toad glanced guiltily at each other. They could see now what a cowardly, even shameful, thing they might have done without Malcolm's remarkable conscience to guide them.

"O.K., Malcolm," said his sister in a remorseful voice. "I can see that you're perfectly right. But the only thing is — I mean — how *are* we going to get along without any money?"

"We'll work and make some, that's how!" her brother explained, pounding his fist enthusiastically on the table and sloshing a little milk out of their glasses.

"I don't suppose — uh — we'll be hungry or anything, will we?" inquired the Toad in a voice which was intended to sound brave, but which had a little quaver at the end.

His sister Molly promptly reached out her small square hand to pat his shoulder. "Heavens, Toad!" she reassured him. "You know how full the storeroom in the basement is! And the freezer, too! And there are boxes and boxes of Dad's vitamin samples all over the house! Why, we could live for years!"

The Toad immediately looked relieved, and actually made the first suggestion about fund raising. "I could sell Nervous's kittens — when she has them," he offered. "They'll really be mine, of course, but everybody can use the money."

At this idea his older brother and sister smiled without much spirit. In the first place, if the kittens looked anything like Nervous, they doubted if anyone would pay anything for such odd, three-colored, patchwork creatures. Secondly, they had been waiting for Nervous to have kittens for nearly a year now — ever since the Toad had picked her out at the pound — and it seemed unwise to count on an event which everybody except the Toad had given up hoping for.

"I could take a morning paper route," mused Malcolm, who already had one in the afternoon. "And I guess the Billiards and the Seemlys will probably want me to cut their grass again this summer — besides Mr. Forthright and Miss Eva."

"But that's just a couple of dollars here and there," said Molly. "What we need is one big project we can all work on! Why don't we speak to Mr. Forthright about it? He's a minister. He ought to know about lots of charity jobs open to poor but honest people."

Malcolm shuddered. "Promise me you won't either of you mention a word of this to Mr. Forthright!" he ordered them.

"Honestly, Malcolm!" Molly remarked. "I don't see why you're so secret about this."

"Because it's our private business, that's why!" replied her brother. "And we're not charity cases! Besides," he added, "Mr. Forthright would only write Dad if we told him we were short of money."

"No, he wouldn't," Molly assured him. "Not if you explained to him about it's being a matter of principle, the way you explained to us!"

But Malcolm shook his head firmly. "I happen to be perfectly sure he would write Dad," he said, though he would not explain how he knew.

And so the three children sat at the table long after their supper was finished and tried to think of ways to earn money. But nothing very exciting occurred to anyone, and after a while the two younger ones began to look fidgety and discouraged. When he noticed this, their older brother reassured them. "There's nothing to worry about! Something will turn up."

"You know," said Molly, getting up and collecting the plates, "it's really an awfully good thing Mrs. Coverlet's not here — since *this* happened. One less mouth to feed, for one thing. And when we *do* find a project or something,

40

it'll be a lot easier to do without a grownup around."

"You're absolutely right!" Malcolm told her approvingly. "We're much better off on our own!"

"Mrs. Coverlet's letter says she'll be away at least another three weeks," Molly reminded them. "She says Marygold's foot is up in traction or something."

"That's good," said Malcolm.

"Good?" the Toad asked. "Does Marygold like — what is it? — traction?"

"Don't be silly, Toad!" Molly told him disapprovingly. "Malcolm merely meant it gives us plenty of time to think about our project and do it."

"Right!" said Malcolm in his manly voice. "All we need to do is think! So think, everybody. Think!"

Chapter VI

THE next morning by ten o'clock all three Persevers were working on Miss Eva Penalty's yard. Malcolm was pushing the lawn mower, Molly was digging crab grass and plantain with a narrow trowel, and the Toad was raking up lawn clippings while Nervous ran about him and rolled in the piles of grass and boxed with the rake. It hadn't been easy for Malcolm to persuade the younger ones to come and help him. "I've got to do Miss Eva's yard this morning," he had told them at breakfast, "and since nobody has thought of a good way to make money yet, why don't you at least come and help me? If she sees that you're really working — not just horsing around the way you usually do — she might pay all of us."

"Well, just this once, then," Molly had agreed. "But I'll bet it'll be just like always. She'll stick her head out and say aren't we darling little children to help our dear

big brother and please keep off the flowers. But no money!"

Sure enough, when the children had been working for only a few minutes, Miss Eva's front door opened, and out she came and stood on her porch. Now, Miss Eva Penalty was a remarkably thin lady with pale eyes that blinked and swam behind her glasses. Over and over, Mr. Forthright had told Malcolm how fond Miss Eva was of children and how lonely she was in her empty house, with no one in the world to look after. Still, I am sorry to say, the Perserver children did not appreciate Miss Eva, and never felt comfortable with her, though she had lived next door to them all their lives and always took the greatest interest in the whole family — particularly the Toad.

"Aren't you good children to come and help your big brother!" she called, smiling and blinking. "Only *do* be careful about stepping in the flower beds!" Molly, on her knees, with the trowel in her hand, gave Malcolm a hard look as he passed her, pushing the mower.

By now Miss Eva's weak eyes had settled on the Toad, and they began to blink more moistly and furiously than ever behind her glasses. She came down off the porch and across the grass toward him. The Toad, thinking about how he would have to go and stay with her, and be scrubbed and loved, and fed Brussels sprouts, if she were ever to find out about Mrs. Coverlet, began to rake the grass over and over in the same spot so violently that you might have thought the point of his work was to pull it all out by the roots.

"Has Nervous had her kittens yet, Theobold?" Miss Eva asked him, bearing down upon the little boy.

"Not today she hasn't — but I think tomorrow maybe," replied the Toad, keeping his eyes on the ground and panting and raking.

"I doubt if she ever has kittens!" came Molly's small, crisp voice from behind a large syringa bush. "I'm beginning to think Nervous is a boy!" What made her say such a thing, she couldn't imagine, for the idea had never

44

entered her head till that very moment. But she was cross with herself for having let Malcolm talk her into coming over to Miss Eva's, and cross with Miss Eva because she was sure that she and the Toad were not going to be paid, and she suddenly wanted to say something irritating and startling.

"Nonsense!" Miss Eva said at once, scowling at the innocent syringa bush. "Of *course* Nervous is a girl! All tortoise-shell cats are girls! Tortoise-shell males are so excessively rare that enormous sums of money are paid for

them by cat fanciers!" She put out her thin hand to smooth the Toad's rumpled hair, which I must admit had not been combed that morning. "By the way," she said, "how is dear Mrs. Coverlet? I haven't talked with her in days. We usually have such nice little chats when she hangs out the clothes. That's when I find out how my mischievous little neighbors are behaving! Well?" she asked as the Toad opened and closed his mouth perfectly silently. "Isn't Mrs. Coverlet all right?"

"Oh — she's — uh, she's — uh" stammered the Toad until Molly came to his rescue at last.

"Mrs. Coverlet's fine!" Molly's cool voice broke in. "As far as we know," she added softly and with perfect truth.

"Well, what can she be thinking of to stay indoors in this exquisite weather?" Miss Eva wanted to know. "Tell her from me to let the housework go!"

"I certainly will!" Molly promised wholeheartedly. "As soon as I see her."

"Did she pay us anything?" Molly asked Malcolm an hour or so later when they had put the garden tools away in Miss Eva's garage and were crossing her yard on their way to have lunch.

"She gave me a dime for each of you," Malcolm muttered, looking a little apprehensively at his sister.

But to his surprise all Molly said was, "It doesn't matter. She may have given us all a lot more than she thought." She stopped and twitched Malcolm's sleeve a little to make

46

him wait beside her, while the Toad went on ahead. "While you were cutting the grass and couldn't hear," she explained, "Miss Eva was saying that boy tortoise-shell cats are very rare and terribly valuable!"

"So what," Malcolm shrugged. "Nervous is a girl. The man at the pound said so."

"Suppose he was wrong?" asked Molly. "A year is a long time for a *her* not to have kittens. Suppose she *is* a he! Suppose somebody would give us a fortune for her — him!"

Malcolm was looking thoughtfully ahead at their little brother, who was just running up the back steps to the kitchen door, carrying Nervous on his shoulder. "He'd never sell Nervous," Malcolm said.

But Molly only shrugged. "Let's not worry about that," she said practically. "The first thing to do is take Nervous to the veterinary and find out!"

Chapter VII

"TOAD," remarked Malcolm in a friendly voice as they were sitting at the kitchen table a few minutes later making themselves a lunch of raisin bread spread thickly with peanut butter and then marshmallow sauce and topped with slices of banana, "what would you think of walking over to see what's going on at Dr. Furry's Animal Hospital this afternoon?"

"Oh, boy!" the unsuspecting Toad cried. "But Nervous wants to go with us this time. Why don't you guys ever let me take her?"

"By all means, bring Nervous!" his sister Molly put in before the Toad's words were well out of his mouth, and she gave him such an agreeable smile that he looked at her in some surprise.

And so, when lunch was over and they had put the tops on the jars of peanut butter and marshmallow and placed the three half-finished glasses of milk back in the refrigerator — for they were being awfully economical these days — the three Persevers started off for Dr. Furry's. And I must say, the two older ones were unusually nice about taking turns helping the Toad carry Nervous, who could get quite heavy and wriggly on a hot summer afternoon.

There was nobody in Dr. Furry's waiting room when they went in. Molly and the Toad sat down in two wicker chairs, with Nervous on the Toad's lap, while Malcolm went over to the counter at the end of the room and rang Dr. Furry's bell. The door behind the counter opened, the veterinary came out, and they could hear a chorus of yelps and howls from his canine patients beyond.

"Don't be so nervous, Nervous!" murmured the Toad soothingly as his cat leaped up out of his lap and perched on his shoulder. "There are only sick, weak dogs here."

"Hello, kids!" Dr. Furry said in a pleased voice when he saw who was there. Dr. Furry was a friend of their father's and the children often came down to visit his hospital. "You've brought a cat, I see! An honest-to-goodness tortoise-shell. What can I —"

"Excuse me, sir," Malcolm interrupted in a low voice. "Could I speak to you a minute — alone?"

"Certainly," the doctor replied, and he lifted the hinged part of the counter, let Malcolm through, and showed him into his private office.

When they came out into the waiting room again a moment later, Dr. Furry came quickly over to the chair where the Toad and Nervous were waiting. "So this is Nervous?" he asked in an interested way, expertly prying the Toad's cat from the little boy's shoulder. "Now, I know you three came down here to look at the animals, so why don't you go on back and let me keep Nervous for you?"

"Nervous wants to come with me," the Toad said. "She thinks she might find a sick friend to visit."

"Oh, I'm sorry, Toad," replied Dr. Furry, "but I can't allow animal visitors in my wards. It's apt to excite some of the patients."

"Heck!" said the Toad. "Well, O.K., then, Nervous. You stay here with Dr. Furry."

After they had looked at all the patients, particularly admiring one Airedale who had his hind leg in a beautiful plaster cast, the children returned to the waiting room. Dr. Furry was sitting there in a wicker chair, a stunned expression on his pleasant face, holding Nervous on his lap, with both hands, as gingerly as if she were an antique lamp.

"Amazing . . . incredible!" he was muttering to himself as the children approached, and he ran one hand respectfully down Nervous's back, while she purred smugly. "I've read about these fellows in textbooks, of course, but never thought I'd ever see one . . . classic markings, too . . . even the blaze across the nose . . . gorgeous!" The

three children leaned forward to get a better look at Nervous's familiar comical nose, which was exactly as they remembered it, a curious sight, half orange and half black.

"I'll take her back now," the Toad said, feeling uneasy as Dr. Furry kept stroking his cat in this odd, dreamy way. He picked Nervous lightly from the veterinary's lap and set her casually on his shoulder.

"Careful!" gasped the doctor, leaping to his feet, with his hands outstretched beneath Nervous. "Careful of him, Toad! He's one in a million! He's absolutely priceless!"

Chapter VIII

"THERE'S one hamburger left," the Toad remarked that night at supper. "Who gets it?"

"You take it, Toad!" Malcolm generously offered.

"Yes, you have it," insisted Molly.

"Remember, I haven't made up my mind about selling Nervous yet," the Toad warned them, quickly reaching out his fork and spearing the hamburger anyway.

"Just — uh, how soon do you think you will make it up?" asked practical Molly. "So we can make plans and all?"

"Soon," said their small brother, squinting his eyes and assuming the intelligent expression he often practiced before the bathroom mirror these days. "I'm making it up now. I *may* be through right after dessert."

Sure enough, when dessert was over — it was chocolate pudding made by Molly and very good — the Toad announced that his mind was made up. Malcolm and Molly put down their spoons quietly and held their breaths.

"I've decided," said the Toad distinctly, "that I won't sell Nervous to *any*body!"

"But, Toad!" groaned his horrified brother and sister together. "You know how import —"

"Just the same," repeated the stubborn child, "I won't sell my cat to just *any*body!"

Malcolm took a deep breath. "Do you mean that you won't sell Nervous to *any*body, Toad? Or do you mean —"

"I mean," the Toad said patiently to his brother and sister, who could not seem to understand the simplest words, "that I won't sell Nervous to anybody — just to somebody I like!"

"Oh-h-h-h!" breathed Malcolm and Molly.

"But," the Toad went on, "even if I like this person, I *still* won't sell Nervous unless Nervous likes him, too!"

"Of course you wouldn't!" Malcolm agreed, pushing back his chair and standing up. "Now that you've decided, I'll go give Dr. Furry a ring. I promised I'd let him know the minute you made up your mind, so he can start looking around for a buyer."

But at this the Toad began to scowl blackly. "I'm not finished yet," he told Malcolm.

"Now what, Toad?" asked Malcolm, sitting down again, reluctantly.

"Even if Dr. Furry can find somebody I like, and even if this person comes here and I see that Nervous likes him — I still won't sell Nervous unless!"

"Unless what, Toad?"

"Well, you know how I've been waiting and waiting for a whole year for Nervous to have kittens? If I could have a mother cat, a *real* mother cat, with *real* kittens, then —"

"Why, of course you can have a mother cat!" Malcolm cried, clapping his little brother affectionately on the back.

"Go call Dr. Furry and tell him it's O.K., Malcolm," Molly said under her breath.

"Sit down, you!" the Toad roared rudely at Malcolm. "I haven't finished yet!"

"Oh, what is it now, Toady?" asked his brother, clenching his fists.

"I don't *have* to sell Nervous, you know!" the Toad growled. "She's my cat, and I'm *very* fond of him!"

Malcolm and Molly looked unhappily at each other. "We'd never ask you to if it weren't the only thing to do," his sister told him gently. "But you know we have to make money, and we haven't been able to think of any other —"

"I know, I know!" the Toad interrupted crossly. "Well, if Nervous is happy with the person who buys her—him— and if I can find the right mother cat — not just *any* mother cat — I want a gray one with blue eyes and white feet and kittens—three or four will do—then I will sell Nervous!"

Everybody sat perfectly quiet for several seconds after the Toad had finished, not daring to move. At last Malcolm meekly asked, "Is that all, Toad? Now can I call Dr. Furry?"

"Sure!" said the Toad, looking at him in surprise. "What are you waiting for?"

Chapter IX

NEXT morning, while the children were eating a leisurely breakfast, Dr. Furry called Malcolm on the phone. "A Mrs. Dextrose-Chesapeake is on her way from New York to see Nervous!" the veterinary said excitedly. "She ought to be there by noon. For heaven's sake, don't lose the cat in the meantime! I'm coming over there myself as soon as I finish feeding my animals! Goodness, I still can't believe it! A genuine male tortoise-shell right here in Loganbury!"

"Who's Mrs. Dextrose-Chesapeake?" Malcolm wanted to know.

"Why, I called the American Cat Club in New York this morning," Dr. Furry told him. "They gave me her name. She's the greatest cat fancier in the country."

"Suppose the Toad doesn't like her?" Malcolm groaned.

"Keep your fingers crossed, my boy! That's all we can do!"

"And what if Nervous doesn't like her?"

"Good lord!" Dr. Furry said impatiently. "The point is, will *she* like Nervous? He's got to be a perfect specimen or she won't be interested. Gosh! There's no white on him, is there? If there is, he's only a calico, not a tortoise-shell, and practically worthless!"

"White?" Malcolm gasped. "No — I'm sure — I mean — I don't think — I never noticed —"

"Keep calm, boy!" shouted Dr. Furry, breathing so heavily into the receiver that it tickled Malcolm's ear. "Just keep calm till I get there! Now, good-by till —"

"Wait, Dr. Furry! Remember the other thing!"

"What other thing?"

"The mother cat! I told you last night! Gray — blue eyes — white feet — kittens! You know!"

"Lord, I'd forgotten! Well, I'll scout around and see what I can do. Does Theobold have to have her today?"

"It certainly would help!"

Dr. Furry sighed. "It's fortunate I mentioned all Theo-

58

bold's conditions to Mrs. Dextrose-Chesapeake on the phone so she'd have an idea what she was getting into. Now I must go feed the patients, Malcolm! They're all howling and meowing and climbing up the cages. Just *don't* lose that *cat!*"

Malcolm immediately went back into the kitchen and told the others about the lady from New York.

"*Mrs.* Dextrose-Chesapeake — Mrs. *Dex*trose-*Ches*apeake . . ." murmured the Toad as he poured some maple syrup thickly over his scrambled eggs.

"Lovely, lovely name, don't you think?" Molly asked him, eying him anxiously.

"Um-m-m-m," mumbled the Toad noncommittally.

The doorbell rang while they were washing the breakfast dishes. "It's Mrs. Dextrose-Chesapeake already!" cried Malcolm, throwing down his dish towel and hurrying to the front door. "Oh, no, it's only Dr. Furry," he called back to the others as he saw their friend the veterinary waiting impatiently on the front porch.

"Listen, Malcolm," he whispered, stepping inside and looking about the empty vestibule. "Where's Theobold?"

"In the kitchen."

"How's he taking everything?"

"Fine. Perfectly calm."

"Well, I couldn't find a mother cat like the kind he wants any place! Called the pound. Called the pet shops. Called the other animal hospitals. I could get a gray mother cat with yellow eyes and white feet, several mother cats with blue eyes and no white feet. Actually I could find any kind of cat you can name, except what he wants!"

"Maybe it won't matter too much," said Malcolm, trying to hide his concern. "I mean, if he knows he can be looking around for a mother cat, and if he likes Mrs. Dextrose-Chesapeake and all."

"Let's hope so!" the veterinary exclaimed. "It's too fantastic a chance to be lost. Why, you kids might make enough money to live on till your father gets home and then some!"

"Remember, sir, you promised you wouldn't say anything about — you know — our being poor, and having to do this, to anybody?"

"Of course not, my boy! No need to if everything goes all right today." Dr. Furry hit his hands together excitedly. "Won't your father get a kick out of this when he gets home?" he chuckled.

60

"I hope so!" Malcolm sighed.

Dr. Furry sat down near the front window in the living room to watch for Mrs. Dextrose-Chesapeake. While they were waiting, there was a sudden loud clatter of dishes in the kitchen. Dr. Furry turned his head that way. "Why, I'd forgotten to say hello to Mrs. Coverlet!" he said. "How is she bearing up under all this excitement? I'll just run out to the kitchen now while we're waiting."

"Oh, don't do that, sir!" Malcolm gasped, turning pale. With so many things on his mind, he'd quite forgotten that Dr. Furry might expect to see Mrs. Coverlet. "She — isn't here at the moment!" he added.

"Mrs. Coverlet isn't here?" asked Dr. Furry in astonishment.

"Something came up," Malcolm told him, "and she had to go out and — uh — take care of it."

Fortunately, that was the very moment when Dr. Furry caught sight of something through the window which made him forget everything else. "It's Mrs. Dextrose-Chesapeake!" he breathed. A long black car had just drawn up before the house. While they watched, a chauffeur got out, came solemnly around the car, and opened the rear door. Out stepped a stout lady in a copper-colored dress, with black hair tightly pulled into a big knot behind her head. She gazed very keenly at the Persevers' house with wise black eyes and then came hurrying up the walk.

"I'm Dr. Furry!" announced the veterinary, coming down the Persevers' front steps to meet Mrs. Dextrose-Chesapeake. He took her arm politely and said, "I called you this morning in New York."

"Yes, indeed, Doctor, and I am grateful to you," Mrs. Dextrose-Chesapeake replied in a strong, unhurried voice.

"And these are the Persever children," continued Dr. Furry, waving his free hand in the direction of the front doorway, where Malcolm, Molly, and the Toad were watching them approach. "I explained to you about their father's being away on business and so forth."

"Yes, you did, Doctor," Mrs. Dextrose-Chesapeake agreed. "How do you do?" she said slowly and seriously to each of the three Persevers as Dr. Furry introduced them.

Then for a moment everybody stood rather awkwardly in the vestibule until matter-of-fact Molly suggested that they go sit down while she got Nervous, and they all went into the living room to wait.

When Molly joined them a minute later, holding a terribly cross and rumpled Nervous, who had been snatched up without a by-your-leave from the roof outside Malcolm's window where he had been sunning himself, Mrs. Dextrose-Chesapeake fixed her black eyes on him and drew in her breath. Molly set him down on Mrs. Dextrose-Chesapeake's broad rust-colored lap, and the lady from New York put her large hand on his head and ran it firmly down his back.

63

"To whom does this wonderful cat belong?" asked Mrs. Dextrose-Chesapeake.

"Me!" the Toad replied. He was sitting all by himself in the middle of the sofa, with his freckled arms folded proudly across his chest.

"Then it's you I must talk to," Mrs. Dextrose-Chesapeake said, looking at him solemnly. With Nervous in her arms she came across the floor and sat down beside the Toad. Then she tilted Nervous's chin up so that she could look into his face. "He is very beautiful, and very funny, too, with his black and orange nose. But I don't have to tell *you* how special he is." And then she smiled at the Toad, the first time she had smiled since she came. It was a wide, plain smile, and when the Toad had studied it for a moment, he smiled back at her.

But then she looked serious again. "Listen, Theobold," she said, "I'm going to tell you the truth. I want to buy your cat, but I can't love Nervous more, or give him a better home, than you can, right here. If he comes to New York," she went on, keeping her black, wise eyes very solemnly on the Toad's little brown face, "he will be very spoiled, and very famous. He'll go to shows, and even have his picture in the papers. But you know," she murmured, smiling again and scratching Nervous on his favorite spot under the ear, "it's been my experience — and I've been a friend of cats for years — that they are all a little vain, a little pleased with themselves, and that they *love* that sort of life!"

The Toad leaned his head back against the sofa and chuckled. "Oh, Nervous is very proud!" he said. "He's always told me he was a special cat! But I thought," he said, looking down at his pet a little sadly and reproachfully, "I thought he meant he was a special *mother* cat!"

"If you let me have him," said Mrs. Dextrose-Chesapeake, "I would have to give you a great deal of money."

"Oh, I know *that*," the Toad nodded smugly, "because you're so rich, and we need money, and Nervous is so valuable."

Molly and Malcolm winced to hear their brother's words. There were times when it seemed to them that their years of trying to raise and civilize him had been a wasted effort.

But Mrs. Dextrose-Chesapeake seemed not in the least embarrassed. "Exactly!" she said to the Toad, nodding at him as if he had said something remarkably clever. "But even if I *do* give you money," she continued, "it can't make up for losing your special pet, can it?" The little Toad looked at Mrs. Dextrose-Chesapeake and blinked, then glanced down at his funny patchwork cat, who was purring on Mrs. Dextrose-Chesapeake's orange lap, and began to scratch his knobby knee in a lonesome way.

Malcolm and Molly and Dr. Furry listened to Mrs. Dextrose-Chesapeake's words in some alarm. It seemed to them terribly unwise of her to begin to talk in this way, when everything had been going so well up to then. But suddenly she was speaking to them. "I wonder if you three would keep Nervous for us, just a minute?" she asked. "Theobold and I are going out to the car to look at something."

"Certainly!" Dr. Furry cried, leaping to his feet and hurrying over to take the reluctant Nervous from Mrs. Dextrose-Chesapeake's roomy lap.

Mrs. Dextrose-Chesapeake and the Toad left the room and went out the front door and down the walk together.

"What're they doing?" Malcolm hissed at Molly, for she was sitting next to the front window.

"They're standing by the car," his sister told him. "The chauffeur just opened the back door . . . they're all looking in. There's a box or something on the back seat. The

Toad's pulling it out. He's got it and he's looking inside it. . . . Wait, they're coming back. . . . I can't see what's in the box . . . but the Toad's carrying it. Shhh! Here they are!"

But only Mrs. Dextrose-Chesapeake came into the living room, and they heard the Toad's steps going slowly up the stairs to his room.

"Is everything all right, Mrs. Dextrose-Chesapeake?" asked Dr. Furry anxiously.

"Quite perfect, thank you," she replied, sitting down on the sofa again. "Oh! Here's my darling!" she laughed as Nervous made a magnificent leap out of Dr. Furry's arms and into her lap, where he began to purr uproariously. "Theobold says I am to give the money to you to look after, Doctor," she said, taking a wallet out of her big black pocketbook.

She counted him out a roll of green bills as thick as a pack of playing cards. Dr. Furry's eyes bulged. "Mrs. Dextrose-Chesapeake," he gasped, "you are most generous!"

"Nonsense," she said. "A cat like Nervous is priceless! Anyway, here is Theobold again!" Malcolm's and Molly's grubby little brother came into the room and sat down close to Mrs. Dextrose-Chesapeake on the couch; whereupon Nervous jumped out of Mrs. Dextrose-Chesapeake's lap and into his.

"Is everything settled upstairs?" Mrs. Dextrose-Chesapeake asked him in a low voice. The Toad gave her a private nod. "Then I'd better be starting home," she said. But first she put out her large square hand, where a large square ring was shining, and touched the Toad's brown hair. "I think Nervous wants *you* to carry him to the car," she said.

"Don't you want a box or something, Mrs. Dextrose-Chesapeake?" Malcolm asked, anxious to be helpful.

"No, thank you, Malcolm," she told him, getting to her feet. "I'm sure Nervous will want to ride beside me and enjoy the countryside."

When Mrs. Dextrose-Chesapeake was settled in her car, she leaned forward and, holding Nervous's checkered head against her cheek, looked out the open window to where the Persevers and Dr. Furry stood on the sidewalk. "Good-by, everyone! Good-by, Toad!" she said. And suddenly she stretched her arm out of the window and took the Toad's hand in hers. "Have you ever been to New York, Theobold?" she asked.

He shook his head.

"Would you like to? There's a cat show the end of this summer. You could stay with me, and we could both go see Nervous in his glory! And there's the zoo, you know, and the parks, and all the boats in the harbor, and — "

"Boy!" the Toad interrupted. "When am I coming?"

"I'll write you," said Mrs. Dextrose-Chesapeake, smiling again, her wide, plain smile, "and let you know when I'm sending the car for you."

"Good-by, Mrs. Dextrose-Chesapeake!" they all called as the big black car began to slip along the street away from them.

"Good-by, my old Nervous!" said the Toad, last of all.

While they were standing together on the sidewalk next to the empty street, Dr. Furry reached into his breast pocket and drew out the stack of bills. "Thirteen hundred dollars!" he whispered, riffling through them incredulously. "Thirteen hundred dollars for *one cat!*" The three children stared at the money with their mouths open.

"We certainly won't have to worry Dad now!" Malcolm said solemnly.

"Maybe we ought to send *him* some," suggested Molly.

"Whatever you do with it, we ought to go put it in the bank this minute," Dr. Furry said. "I don't like the responsibility."

"Oh, not yet!" the Toad said, pulling Dr. Furry's arm. "I want to show you guys something first." So they all started back to the house, and the Toad ran ahead. By the time they were indoors they heard his voice calling from above, "Up here! In my room!"

He was kneeling in front of a box on the floor as they came in and peered over his head. Inside lay a little

70

gray cat, with a coat as pale and bright as lavender. Each of her feet was tipped with white, like four dancing sandals. She watched them calmly with clear blue eyes. "Her name is Heather," the Toad whispered. "She was Mrs. Dextrose-Chesapeake's pet."

And then, as he drew back his head a little from over the box, they could see five tiny breathing crescents of fur, two gray, two white, and one pure black, all neatly folded against each other.

"Kittens!" sighed the Toad. "Finally, I've got kittens!"

Chapter X

DOES it seem strange to you that the three Persever children could live in their house without a grownup in charge, and have no one suspect it? Actually it was easier than the children had thought it would be. The neighbors all assumed that Mrs. Coverlet was with them, because it had never entered any of their heads to suppose that she wouldn't be. That they had always been such independent, capable children and had come and gone pretty much as they pleased was another thing that helped.

Mr. Romaine, the grocer, thought nothing of seeing them come into his store every few days with a list, for they had been carrying home Mrs. Coverlet's orders for years. Once, though, he did give them a scare by remarking, "Aren't you eating anything at your place this summer except hamburg and chocolate ice cream? Doesn't sound like Mrs. Coverlet's style of cooking to me!" But the store had been crowded when he said it, and afterwards he only laughed, handed them their packages, and turned to the next customer.

It was true that they relied pretty heavily on hamburgers, varied occasionally with chops. This was partly because roasts and stews were complicated to fix, but mostly because these things had to be started such a long time before you wanted to eat them. Indeed, the main difference between the way the children did the cooking and Mrs. Coverlet's way was that they never thought about a meal until they were hungry, while, with Mrs. Coverlet, things were perpetually baking or stewing or mixing or cooling, even at the most unhungry times of day.

On the whole, the Persevers managed very well. They took turns (with scarcely any serious arguing) doing the cleaning, and cooking, and washing. "Everybody knows what a good housekeeper Mrs. Coverlet is," Malcolm told the others shortly after she had gone. "The way to make anyone who comes in suspect about things would be for them to find the place a mess!"

So they were faithful about the vacuum, the mop, and the scouring powder. And it seemed to them that the house looked just as tidy as it always had.

About four o'clock one afternoon in July, when it was the Toad's turn to make supper, Malcolm opened the kitchen door to find the air there simply shimmering with the most remarkable odor. It was meaty, flowery, crackling, tender, and silky all at once; a smell which Malcolm's nose instantly told him was the very smell it had been looking for and dreaming of all its young life.

"Gosh, Toad!" Malcolm murmured, overcome. "What's for supper?"

"The usual," replied the Toad, who was standing by the stove. "Hamburgers. But I haven't started them yet."

Malcolm, coming over to the stove, saw that his small brother was stirring a thick purplish syrup in a saucepan. Now and then a bubble on its glistening surface would break, and then Malcolm's nose, which he was suspending no more than an inch above the syrup, would quiver with joy, as a fresh wave of the fascinating scent arose to meet it.

"What is it? What's in it?" the oldest Persever kept repeating in a trancelike voice as he crouched blissfully over the saucepan.

"It's cat food," answered his brother shortly. "Hey, get your head out of it, will you, Malcolm! I can't see what I'm doing."

But Malcolm, only dimly aware of the Toad's prodding elbow, went on sniffing and sighing. "What's it really, Toady? Come on, Toad!"

"It's just a little something I'm mixing up for Heather,"

the Toad insisted. "You wouldn't like it, Malcolm."

"What's it made of?"

"Diffront things, diffront things," muttered the unhelpful child, who now gave Malcolm a particularly hard poke in the ribs. "Move over, will you! It's ready now and I have to take it off and cool it." He lifted the pan from the stove and carried it across the room. Malcolm's nose, with the rest of Malcolm close behind it, followed the saucepan, keeping directly in its trail of steam.

The Toad set the pan on a shelf near the open window and stirred it slowly to help it cool. "Heather is a very fussy eater, you know," he explained to his brother. "Not like Nervous. Nervous was always hungry. Mrs. Dextrose-Chesapeake told me I'd have to tempt Heather's appetite. So today I thought I'd just invent something — kind of a sauce, you know — to pour on her supper to tempt her."

"Is there anything in it a person couldn't eat?" Malcolm inquired.

His brother gave him an offended look. "Do you think I'd put poison in my cat's supper?" he demanded crossly. "It's just got regular things in it — mostly."

"I have to get Heather for her supper now," the Toad informed Malcolm after the sauce had cooled. He brought in his cat in his arms and set her down on the kitchen floor in front of her usual supper of canned fish. But the dainty little cat gave her dinner a bored sniff, sat back on her silky tail, and looked up reproachfully at the Toad. "Never mind, Heather," he told her, "just wait till you taste *this!*" He poured a few spoonfuls of his purple sauce over the cat food. The change in the little cat was electrifying! Her long pale whiskers, which always dipped so gracefully and languidly, stood straight out like silver wires. Her gentle blue eyes flashed as fiercely as the sapphires on an Arabian warrior's turban. She gobbled down her supper with no more manners than Nervous himself.

"That's better!" murmured the Toad, squatting beside her and hugging his bony little knees with satisfaction. When she was through, he picked Heather up. "I have to

76

take her back to her babies now," he explained to Malcolm. "Then I'll start the hamburgers, since you're so hungry."

As soon as Malcolm was alone in the kitchen, he stretched out a finger to take a taste of the Toad's invention, but at that very minute Molly burst in at the back door. "What's the Toad making for supper?" she panted. "You can smell it clear over at the Billiards'. Mrs. Billiard said it was shrimp curry — and Mr. Billiard said Mrs. Coverlet must be baking apple pies!"

"It's this purple stuff," Malcolm told her. "Something the Toad made to tempt Heather's appetite."

"What on earth has he put in it?" Molly demanded, hovering near the saucepan and taking gulping breaths.

But Malcolm only shook his head. "He wouldn't say," he told her sadly. Later, when they sat down to their own supper, Malcolm took a long, mournful look at his hamburgers, canned peas, and bread and butter, and had not the heart to pick up his fork. It was not that he wasn't hungry, or that the Toad had not cooked things right; it was just that he'd eaten that very same supper so many, many times in the last weeks. And all the while, out of the corner of his eye, he could see the pan of the Toad's sauce on the shelf by the window. "I wonder," he remarked casually, "how you think that sauce would be on a hamburger, Toad?"

The Toad merely shrugged. "Well, don't use it all up!"

he said inhospitably. "It's pretty hard to make, you know, and I want it to last Heather for a while."

Molly looked horrified. "You certainly aren't going to put that stuff on your supper when you don't know what's in it!" she gasped as Malcolm brought the saucepan to the table and poured about a spoonful of it over his meat. "He's probably used mothballs or floor wax!"

At her words the Toad stuck out his lower lip and beetled his brow in a fierce and stubborn expression.

"Yes, why won't you tell us what's in it, Toad?" demanded Malcolm in exasperation, his fork poised over his plate.

"Because I don't *have* to, that's why," snarled their disrespectful brother. "Nobody asked you guys to eat it!" I must say the Toad was getting unbearably bold! Ever since he had sold Nervous for thirteen hundred dollars, he had thought nothing of saying whatever he pleased to his brother and sister, regardless of their greater age and intelligence. And things had gotten even worse in the last few days, ever since the letter had come from Mrs. Dextrose-Chesapeake telling him she was sending her car for him on August 27 to take him back to New York for a visit.

Malcolm looked first at his unmanageable brother, then at his hamburger. But finally he put a piece of it on his fork and took a bite. Molly stared, and the Toad paid no attention whatsoever.

78

"Well, what's it like?" Molly asked curiously.

There was no reply from Malcolm. He merely picked up the saucepan and poured the purple sauce like gravy over everything on his plate.

"Good gracious!" Molly gasped, watching Malcolm's supper rapidly disappear. The smell of the Toad's invention was tickling her nose like a blend of roses and French-fried onions! "It doesn't seem to be hurting you," she had to admit, watching her older brother closely as he scraped his plate clean and leaned back in his chair with a peaceful smile. "Maybe I'd better try a drop."

So she dipped a teaspoon carefully into the pan and daintily put a drop on the end of her tongue. A smile spread slowly over her face. "Whatever it is," she said, turning respectfully to the Toad, "it's out of this world!" And picking up the saucepan, she poured Heather's appetizer generously on her own dinner.

When she set it down at last, the Toad picked up the empty pan and gloomily surveyed its sticky bottom. "Greedies!" he rudely growled. "Now look what you've done! I've got to make another batch tonight for Heather's breakfast!"

Chapter XI

"I'M going to mow Mr. Forthright's grass," Malcolm called to the Toad next afternoon, coming down the back steps into the hot sun and across the lawn to where his little brother was stretched out in the shade of their chestnut tree. Heather and her five kittens were with the Toad, each of them resting on, or under, or against, some part of the little boy, as if he were a specially constructed cat sofa. All six of them were purring. The Toad's eyes were closed, and the black kitten's tail was resting across his upper lip like a lopsided mustache.

"I was wondering," Malcolm began, looking down at his brother and interrupting this peaceful scene. "I was wondering if I could take this jar of your sauce over to Mr. Forthright's with me?" He held out a jelly glass full of purple sauce. But the Toad refused to open his eyes. He only squeezed them shut as tight as he could and pretended

not to hear. Malcolm went on. "Mr. Forthright mentioned to me this morning that somebody left a meat loaf on his back porch for him, and he hates meat loaf. He says he's got to eat it, though, because whichever lady made it will ask him about it after church on Sunday. And he can't lie, you know, and say he did eat it if he didn't. So I thought about your sauce, and I'm sure it will make the meat loaf a lot easier on Mr. Forthright."

The Toad suddenly let out his breath in a loud, cross way, which slid both the gray kittens off his chest. At this, all six cats stopped purring and looked up accusingly at Malcolm. "I just hope you left some, is all!" the Toad grumbled. The two gray kittens crawled angrily back up on his chest and folded their tiny legs under them once again. All the cats stared coldly at Malcolm as he walked away toward Mr. Forthright's house.

After supper that night, Molly sat down in the living room to read to the Toad, as she did every evening, in her effort to improve him mind. The Toad had asked to hear *The Little Mashed Girl.*

"Not *Mashed Girl, Match Girl*," Molly sighed halfheartedly — because actually there was no use trying to tell the Toad anything nowadays. They had just opened the book when there was a knock at the front door and Malcolm let in Mr. Forthright, terribly out of breath.

"Where's Mrs. Coverlet?" the minister panted. The three children turned pale. Mr. Forthright started toward the kitchen, but Malcolm quickly planted himself in the way. "I've got to see her," continued their friend, "and find out where she got that sauce!"

"Didn't you like it, sir?" Malcolm asked him, standing firmly in his way and trying desperately to think of something to tell Mr. Forthright about Mrs. Coverlet which would be true and at the same time harmless.

"That's just it! It's delicious! If I always had some handy, I could eat anything the ladies sent me and tell them I'd enjoyed it, with a clean conscience. Now, excuse me, old fellow," he said, trying patiently to ease past Malcolm, "I've got to see Mrs. Coverlet!"

"But, sir, Mrs. Coverlet isn't in the kitchen!"

"She isn't? Has she gone to bed already? Why, it's still light out!"

"She gets pretty tired by the end of the day," Malcolm told him with perfect honesty. Indeed, there was not the least doubt in Malcolm's mind that Mrs. Coverlet was tired at this very moment in Duluth, after looking after twin babies and Marygold all day, and getting supper for John, her son-in-law.

"Well, then, I certainly wouldn't want to disturb her," Mr. Forthright said. "I can catch her tomorrow."

"Oh, you don't need to bother to do that, Mr. Forthright," Molly spoke up. "We can tell you anything you want to know about the sauce."

"That's right, sir," agreed Malcolm. "For one thing, you can't buy it. It's — homemade."

"I thought it must be! Do you think Mrs. Coverlet would give me her recipe?"

Molly glanced uneasily at the Toad. "There isn't exactly a recipe," she said. "It's sort of a — family dish."

"What do you call it?" Mr. Forthright wanted to know. "You must have a name for something so unusual."

Molly and Malcolm looked blank, but the Toad, who had not said a word since Mr. Forthright came in, announced calmly, "It's called Heather's Temptation."

"Perfect! Heather's Temptation!" Mr. Forthright nodded his head and repeated the name happily to himself several times. "Well, I can't stay," he said at last. "I'm working on my sermon tonight. Tell Mrs. Coverlet I stopped by." As he started for the front door, all three children politely, you might even say eagerly, escorted him.

"We'll bring you down some more sauce any time you want!" Malcolm called after him from the doorway.

"Thank you, I'd appreciate it!" Suddenly, on the last step of the porch, the minister stopped and looked around. "Why, I've just had an inspiration!" he cried. "Do you suppose we could get a few bottles of Heather's Temptation for the church bazaar?"

The children shifted their weight uncomfortably in the doorway.

"You know, we count on Mrs. Coverlet's apple pies every year," he explained. "As a matter of fact, I was going to come up and see her about the bazaar in the next day or two. But this Heather's Temptation is such an extraordinary thing, I'm sure it would be a tremendous hit. If you wouldn't mind asking her if we could have a batch of it, I'd appre —"

"Count on us, Mr. Forthright!" Malcolm called reassuringly. "We'll see that you get some for the bazaar!"

"Oh, *yeah?*" came the outraged voice of the Toad behind him. "Hey, what do — " But here Molly hastily put her hand over his mouth while Malcolm closed the front door.

"Since when do I have to make my cat sauce for all the people at the church bazaar?" demanded the Toad, now that they were alone, furiously wriggling out of Molly's hold.

Malcolm, turning from the door, looked down sternly at his brother. *"Now listen to me, Toad!"* he said, so slowly and severely that even Molly looked at Malcolm with awe. The oldest Persever folded his arms and frowned and waited majestically for his small brother to stop twitching and muttering to himself.

"Ever since we sold Nervous, you've been entirely too independent," said Malcolm at last. "Now, we all know that Nervous was your pet, and we appreciated your giving him up. And the result of it is we've got plenty of money, and you have a mother cat and kittens, and you're going to New York in a couple of weeks. But," he added, knitting his brows, "you've gotten so pleased with yourself lately, you've forgotten the main thing!"

"What main thing?" demanded the Toad, jutting his lower lip out disrespectfully.

"I am speaking," Malcolm told him grimly, "of Miss Eva Penalty!" The Toad drew in his lower lip and turned pale. "It doesn't matter to Molly and me whether you make Heather's Temptation for the church bazaar," Malcolm went on. "To tell you the truth, I'd be only too glad if you went down right now and told Mr. Forthright that Mrs. Coverlet's not here and it was you who invented Heather's Temptation. All these weeks have been plenty hard on my conscience. So any time you want to go over and stay with Miss Eva will be a load off my mind." And here Malcolm sighed deeply and marched past his little brother into the living room, without a backward glance at him. Molly, however, shot a disapproving look at the Toad and followed Malcolm.

Then the Toad, left all alone in the empty vestibule, looked down at his sneakers and thoughtfully wiggled his big toes around in the holes. A moment later he hurried into the living room. "I've changed my mind," he announced in a casual voice. "I guess I don't mind making a little extra sauce after all!"

Chapter XII

Dear Malcolm and All [went the letter from Mrs. Coverlet which Malcolm was reading aloud at the breakfast table],

The twins keeping good, and growing, Lord be praised! Marygold's leg is in plaster yet, though the doctors say she's mending fine. Not an hour goes by that I don't think of you. Does the Reverend mind staying nights with you two big ones? Surely he thinks me a wicked soul to have gone off and left you without a word to him. If your dear father gets back before me and finds the house in a state, how will he forgive me? Are you at all looking after things? Change your sheets, for mercy's sake, and take a mop to the kitchen floor. No telling when I'll be back, more's the pity. Thanks be to heavens Theobold is in good hands at Miss Eva Penalty's, where I know he's getting the scrubbing he needs every day!

Bless you all,
Nora Coverlet

"Poor Mrs. Coverlet!" Malcolm remarked sympathetically as he folded the paper. "Too bad she can't be easier in her mind about us. By the way, Toad, when *did* you have a bath last?"

"Pass the syrup," replied the Toad, ignoring the question.

"I'll read Dad's note, too," Molly offered, handing the syrup bottle to the Toad and picking up the postcard from New Zealand.

Dear Kids,

No time for a real letter, but this will let you know I'm well. The mine still has problems to lick, and I could get done a lot quicker with some better equipment. Wonder how the money I left in the bank for you is holding out? Mr. Vault said he'd write if it got low. Haven't heard from him, so you must be managing. Miss you all. Best to Mrs. Coverlet and the neighbors.

Love,
Dad

"Why don't we send Dad some of the money from Nervous to buy new equipment with?" Molly asked.

Malcolm shook his head. "If we do that, we'll be right back where we were. Mr. Vault would write Dad that we were low on money, and Dad would be all confused about where we'd ever gotten so much to send him in the first place. You see, Mr. Vault thinks that the thirteen hundred dollars we put in his bank came from Dad, and he'd think something was crazy if we took it out and sent it to New Zealand."

"I see what you mean," Molly regretfully agreed.

After breakfast had been cleared away, they set off for Mr. Romaine's grocery store to lay in supplies. The minute Mr. Romaine caught sight of the Persevers coming through his glass door, he rushed out from behind the cash register to greet them. "I've called Mrs. Coverlet on the phone three times in the last fifteen minutes!" he said. "And there's no answer."

"She must be out, I guess," suggested Malcolm in his politest voice.

"Apparently," the grocer nodded. "What I wanted to tell her was that I bought some of her superb sauce at the church bazaar the other night. Now, I've been in the food business for thirty-five years, and I never tasted anything to match it. My wife cooks liver at our house once a week, because she says it's good for the kids. I hate liver, but of course I have to eat it to set a good example. Well, with that sauce on it, I simply couldn't get enough! What I want to know is, would Mrs. Coverlet be interested in making me some of her — what did Reverend Forthright tell me you call it — ?"

"Heather's Temptation," prompted Molly.

"Oh, yes — Heather's Temptation. I'd like to sell it here at the store. It would be good for my business, and give her a tidy little sum besides."

While they listened to this idea, Malcolm looked doubtful, and the Toad stuck out his lower lip and turned a hideous maroon.

But practical Molly immediately inquired, "How much could you get for a bottle?"

"We'd better call you about it, Mr. Romaine," Malcolm put in quickly, giving Molly a little kick with his foot.

Later, when they were walking home with their packages, Molly brought the matter up again with some annoyance. "What's eating you, Malcolm?" she asked. "It's a perfect idea to make sauce for Mr. Romaine! We've been looking for a project all summer, and there aren't any grownups around to bother us. Why, we could have a regular factory in the kitchen! It's perfect!"

"Why should we want to make any more money?" Malcolm wanted to know. "We've still got over a thousand dollars left from Nervous."

"For Dad, of course!" Molly exclaimed, astonished at the plodding way Malcolm's mind worked. "We could send him all our profits for his mine. He said in his card this morning how much easier it would be if he had more equipment."

"You'll never get the Toad to do it," Malcolm whispered, looking ahead at their little brother, who was marching along defiantly a few feet in front of them. "Remember how hard it was to get him to make that one extra batch for the church bazaar?"

90

"Yeah!" agreed the Toad, who had been listening to everything they were saying, of course. "And now you want me to be standing over the stove making cat food all day!"

"Not cat food — Heather's Temptation," Molly hastily corrected him.

"Cat food!" insisted the Toad. "I ought to know what it is! I invented it!"

"For heaven's sake!" Molly exclaimed bitterly. "I should think you'd be glad to do something for Dad — it might even bring him home faster — instead of griping about it! If you're too lazy to do it, Toad, why Malcolm and I will make the sauce. Just tell us how you — "

"EN — OH — NO!" shouted the Toad. "I won't tell anybody how to make it. It's my private invention."

Malcolm shrugged and looked at his sister as if to say, "You see? What did I tell you?" And Molly sighed deeply as she looked over the top of her brown paper grocery sack at the Toad's angry red neck. And she thought what a pity it was that all their good money-making ideas — first Nervous and now this — should have to depend upon the cooperation of their unreasonable little brother.

When at last they were back in their own kitchen again, everyone was perspiring from the long walk, and quite cross with everyone else, as they put away the groceries. Only the Toad appeared calm and cheerful as he opened some new peanut butter and, for his midmorning snack, spread it about an inch thick on a piece of pumpernickel. After that he brought out a box of raisins and stuck twenty or thirty of them into the peanut butter so that they formed a large capital T. "Oh, by the way," he remarked, turning his creation around in his hands and admiring it from all sides, "I've decided I will make sauce for Mr. Romaine's store."

"Good old Toad!" Malcolm beamed.

"Starting when?" asked Molly, leaning eagerly across the kitchen table toward him.

"Right after lunch. There's just one thing, though. I don't want anybody hanging around watching me."

"Whatever you say, Toad," Malcolm agreed. But Molly couldn't help fuming a little at this silliness of the Toad's. "Do you need any supplies?" continued Malcolm. "I'll go down to Mr. Romaine's and get them."

The Toad leaned back in his kitchen chair, looked up at the ceiling, and thought for a minute as he munched on his sandwich. "Well," he said, "if I'm going to make a big bunch of it, I'll need a couple of bottles of grape juice, and ketchup, and — uh — some celery salt, and lots of molasses, and some of those soup cubes, and — "

"Goodness, Toad," Molly pointed out with a superior smile, "you might just as well tell us how you make Heather's Temptation. You're already telling us what goes in it!"

92

But here the Toad lowered his gaze from the kitchen ceiling, pressed down a raisin which was slipping off its mattress of peanut butter, and looked sideways at his sister. "What makes you think I'm telling you everything I put in?" he asked craftily.

Molly frowned. This was not the first time she had wondered if there might be something peculiar about the Toad's sauce. Still, it couldn't be anything too awful, because Heather was thriving on it (there'd never been a cat so sleek and fat), the five kittens lapped it up four times a day, mixed with their weaning food, and she and both brothers and most of Mr. Forthright's congregation had tried it with no ill effects. And so she decided it was probably just a trick of the Toad's to make himself seem important, and the disgusting part of it was, there was nothing for her or Malcolm to do but humor him.

Chapter XIII

EVEN the children were amazed at the success of Heather's Temptation. After the first day or so, Mr. Romaine could not keep enough of it on hand to satisfy his customers. Every morning after breakfast, the Toad would brew a fresh batch in absolute privacy. When he was through, Molly took charge of the bottling and labeling. It was a pleasure to see her pour the sticky syrup into rows of clean jars without spilling a drop, then glue a label with HEATHER'S TEMPTATION in pale lavender crayon and in her best printing on each one. Malcolm was the business manager. Besides keeping track of their profits, he delivered the sauce to Mr. Romaine and brought home fresh ingredients and cartons of new jars. The three of them were terribly busy; the hot summer days flew by, and they kept getting richer and richer.

At the grocery store one August afternoon, Mr. Romaine

hurried over to help Malcolm bring in the latest carton of sauce. "Here you are at last!" he exclaimed. "Let me help you there, boy! Listen, Malcolm," he added as he set the case on the floor and began to pull out the jars and arrange them on a shelf. "I wish you'd tell Mrs. Coverlet we can use twice the amount she's sending. People are clamoring for it! They even try to tell me they feel better after eating Heather's Temptation for a while. Yesterday, old Mrs. Renskeller walked down to the store here to get a bottle of it. Yes, I said *walked!* She hasn't set foot out of her house in a year, she's so poorly. Told me she felt as frisky as a young colt, and she lays it all to the bottle of Heather's Temptation her daughter brought over to her for a treat last week."

"I don't know about making any more sauce than this every day," Malcolm said doubtfully. It seemed to him they were already working at full capacity.

Mr. Romaine sighed. "It certainly would be wonderful to be able to talk to Mrs. Coverlet in person about all this! I've never known a person so hard to reach! I never thought of her as being such a shy woman, did you, boy?"

At this turn in the conversation Malcolm decided it was an excellent time to leave. But he had gone only a step or two when Mr. Romaine called after him, "Before you go, Malcolm, here's the money for this week's sauce — fifty-five dollars exactly. You're sure Mrs. Coverlet doesn't

mind your carrying this kind of cash around with you all the time? I could always make her out a check."

"Oh, no, sir!" Malcolm replied earnestly. "Honestly, Mrs. Coverlet never gives a thought to my carrying this money!"

When Malcolm reached the house again and was coming along the path to the back door, he saw Molly in the clothes yard hanging out a few of the Toad's T shirts which she had just washed. "Miss Eva was on the phone a minute ago," she called to him. "She says for you not to mow her grass today. She's going to do it herself."

"Do it herself?" Malcolm gasped, stopping in his tracks. "Is she mad at me about something?"

"No, she says she just feels so bouncy she can't sit still, and she thinks it might be fun to push the lawn mower. Listen!" Molly cocked her yellow head toward Miss Eva's house. "That must be her now!" Sure enough, beyond the chestnut tree they heard the furious whirring of blades. Around the corner of her house Miss Eva came racing, with twinkling heels, behind her lawn mower. When she saw the two Persevers staring at her, she stopped short just opposite them, on the other side of the begonia bed which separated their properties.

"Couldn't resist it, Malcolm," she called apologetically, panting, and blinking her eyes behind her glasses as fast as revolving fans. "It's the Heather's Temptation that's doing it! I bought a bottle last week, and I've had it on my yoghurt every night before retiring. And now I've got more zip, more vim, than in twenty years! Look out for those begonias, Molly! The minute I'm through with this yard I'm coming over to speak to Mrs. Coverlet and get the recipe. My land! Good friends and neighbors as she and I are, there's no reason I should have to go out and *buy* her sauce!"

"She won't be in this afternoon, ma'am," Malcolm said quickly.

"But I'll be glad to bring you over a jar of sauce," added Molly.

A funny look was settling on Miss Eva Penalty's narrow face. "I may as well tell you," she said crisply, "that I intend to have a long talk with your dear father, when he gets back, about Mrs. Coverlet's shocking behavior this summer. And you may tell Mrs. Coverlet I said so! I dare say he'll be very interested to know what went on in his absence! Out all the time! Running around, heaven knows where, and leaving you helpless children to look after yourselves. I declare, I wonder when she's ever home these days! I never catch her! I've said right along that Theobold should have been sent over to me when your father left. Where he'd be properly looked after." All of a sudden her indignant, beating eyelids froze wide apart. "Why, just *look* at that!" she cried. "Dear little

Theobold's shirts! Does Mrs. Coverlet call *that* clean? They look as if a child had tried to wash them!"

Here Molly blushed deeply, but Miss Eva was too busy gazing in horror at the shirts to notice. "Outrageous!" she muttered. "What ghastly neglect!"

But now, even as Molly and Malcolm stared at Miss Eva with a sort of terrified fascination, waiting for her to guess the truth, the Toad's remarkable sauce came to their rescue. Miss Eva apparently felt a sudden burst of energy, for she quivered all over and announced, "Well, I can't just stand here!" She seized the handle of the lawn mower with both hands, lowered her head, and plunged after the mower as fast as she could go. And it would have seemed a funny sight to Malcolm and Molly if they had not been so alarmed by Miss Eva's words.

"It won't be long now," Molly sighed as Miss Eva disappeared around the corner of her porch. "She's getting suspicious. And just when everything is going so well, and we're getting so rich!"

"Poor Toad," Malcolm said sorrowfully as they made their way back to the house. "After all the trouble we've gone to, won't it be a shame if he ends up at Miss Eva's anyway?"

"Not only that," added practical Molly. "The worst of it is, we can't make the sauce without him!"

Chapter XIV

"TWO hundred, two hundred and fifty-two, two hundred and seventy-five. We've made two hundred and seventy-five dollars so far," Malcolm announced to his brother and sister next morning at breakfast. Then he carefully stuffed all the bills back into the brown envelope where he kept them. "As soon as we get three hundred, we'll send it all to Dad." And at this happy thought he leaned back in his chair and began to think about the sort of letter which they ought to send along with the money.

"Dear Dad," it might say, in a modestly casual way. "We've started quite a successful little business here this summer, and we are sending along our profits to you for the mine. It's not much, but here are three hundred dollars to start with, and we hope, later — " Unfortunately, in the midst of these pleasant reflections, the Toad sighed so loudly and dismally that Malcolm blinked, and he

100

and Molly looked in surprise at their little brother.

"What's the matter, Toad? Don't you feel well?" Molly asked, noticing that he had not touched his scrambled eggs and maple syrup. The Toad nodded faintly.

"Better hurry up and eat, then," Malcolm advised. "You've got to get started on the sauce. Promised Mr. Romaine a case of it by noon." But at this the Toad only pushed his favorite breakfast away altogether and sank so low in his chair that nothing but his rumpled brown hair and two unhappy eyebrows were to be seen over the table.

"What is it, Toad?" demanded his older brother and sister, now seriously alarmed.

"Sauce — " croaked the Toad — "can't make — not — any more —"

"Can't *what?*" Molly cried. "Can't *make* Heather's Temptation?"

The bit they could see of the top of the Toad's head was feebly nodding.

"Now listen to me, Toad!" Molly said, speaking reasonably and calmly, and fixing her eyes sternly on this wisp of unruly hair. "It's perfectly silly of you to crouch there out of sight and tell us you can't make sauce when we know you can, and yesterday Malcolm brought home a big supply of grape juice and ketchup and stuff!"

At this, the Toad's head disappeared entirely. "Yuh

— but — but there's something else that has to go in it!"

"Ah, *ha!*" exclaimed Molly. "I always suspected it!"

"And now — it's — all — all gone — used up —"

"Why, that's nothing to worry about, Toad!" Malcolm reassured him. "I'll go out and buy some more. What is the stuff, anyhow?"

A muffled sigh from under the table was his only reply. Then a miserable voice said, "You can't. You see — it was — all those boxes and boxes of Dad's vitamin samples."

"You put Dad's samples of Vitabounce into Heather's Temptation?"

"Uh-huh. I melted down a couple of bottles of them for every batch. The insides of the pills gave the sauce that sort of meaty taste — and the gluey orange stuff on the outsides — well, that made it thick and shiny-looking." There was absolutely no sound from above, and the Toad's voice went on plaintively. "All *I* wanted was just a little something to tempt Heather's appetite. How should I know everybody in town would want to eat cat food!"

"Vitamin pills," Malcolm murmured dazedly. "So that's why they're all cutting their own grass!"

"What's the matter with us, anyway!" Molly exclaimed, suddenly recovering herself and thinking sensibly again, as was her nature. "Why can't we just buy some more vitamins and go on making Heather's Temptation?"

102

At this beautifully simple suggestion, the Toad's head came partly into view again as far as his eyes.

Unfortunately, the first thing he saw was Malcolm shaking his head. "Afraid not," the oldest Persever told the others. "Vitamins are awfully expensive. Gosh, at fifty cents a bottle for Heather's Temptation, people were probably getting over a dollar's worth of melted vitamins! No," he sighed, "this is the end of Heather's Temptation." The Toad's head hastily disappeared.

"You're positive you've used all the samples up?" Molly asked, addressing her little brother's empty chair. "You know there were some boxes in the linen closet upstairs —"

"I know, I know, I know," the Toad's cross voice assured her. "And some in the storeroom, and on the floor of the coat closet. They're all gone — all gone —"

A dreadful silence fell over the kitchen. "I know you guys are mad at me," said the Toad's grumpy but quavering voice. "But you *made* me make it!" Since neither Malcolm nor Molly was really sure whether they were mad at the Toad or not, they looked questioningly at each other, and both of them could see that the other was not.

Suddenly Malcolm burst out laughing. He pounded his fist cheerfully on the table over the place where he thought the Toad's head must be. "Come on up! It doesn't matter,

103

Toad. We'll send Dad all the sauce money we've made so far and take a rest till school starts. It's only another few weeks. This sauce business was an awful lot of work, anyhow." Up came the Toad's face, looking damp and hot, but greatly relieved. He promptly reached for his plate of cold eggs and syrup and ate them greedily.

"Malcolm! What are we *ever* going to tell Mr. Romaine?" Molly suddenly asked in dismay.

"There's nothing to tell," he told her calmly. "I'll just say, 'Sorry, Mr. Romaine, there'll be no more sauce.' "

"You're sure it'll be that simple? He really counts on it, you know. It brings him a lot of extra business, because people come in to get it, and buy a lot of other stuff there, too."

"Of course it will be that simple," Malcolm informed her impatiently. "Mr. Forthright says the truth is always simple! 'Mr. Romaine, sir,' I'll say, 'sorry, but that is the last of the sauce.' "

"Hm-mm," said Molly, looking annoyingly unconvinced. "I hope you're right, Malcolm. I certainly hope he'll be satisfied as easily as you say."

Chapter XV

"WHAT shall we do today, now that we don't have to work?" Malcolm asked a few minutes later when they had left the breakfast table and were standing on the back porch to see what kind of day it was. It was a dry, sweet August morning, and the whole summer day stretched before them perfectly free — no sauce to make, or bottle, or label; no ingredients to carry home; not even any lawns to cut (they thought it would be a week at least until Malcolm's customers had worn off the effects of Heather's Temptation).

"I know what let's do!" the Toad said. "Since we have to go down to Mr. Romaine's anyway and tell him about the sauce, let's ask him for some smelly meat from his trash cans and go turtle hunting with it. We haven't been to the slough all summer!" It was a wonderful idea even if it was only the Toad's! So everybody hurried to put on

105

slough clothes — blue jeans and sneakers — and while Molly and the Toad packed a good supply of peanut butter sandwiches, Malcolm went out to the garage to fish down the turtle net from the rafters.

"Hi, Mr. Romaine!" the three children called brightly as they came out of the sun into the cool store.

"Could we have a little of your bad meat, please?" asked the Toad, at which Mr. Romaine blinked peculiarly.

"Oh, excuse me, Mr. Romaine," Molly hurriedly put in. "He means the meat trimmings in the trash cans, for turtling in the slough, you know."

But Mr. Romaine, still looking strangely at them, came hurrying around the counter without answering. "Where's the sauce? Where's the sauce?" he asked. They were quite empty-handed, except for a sandwich sack and the net on Malcolm's shoulder.

"I'm afraid there won't be any more sauce," Malcolm told the grocer with a serene and pleasant smile.

"No more sauce? No *sauce*, did you say? But three ladies have been in here asking for it already this morning. I told them to come back around noon. Mrs. Seemly's little boy won't eat his oatmeal without it, you know!" said Mr. Romaine, looking reproachfully at Malcolm, as if seeing that Bobby Seemly ate a decent breakfast was clearly Malcolm's responsibility.

"That's a shame," Malcolm agreed, "but —"

"Is it the money? Why, if Mrs. Coverlet feels that fifty cents a bottle isn't enough, we'll raise the price. How about sixty cents a bottle, or even seventy-five? I don't want a penny of it! I'm satisfied just to have the extra business Heather's Temptation brings me!"

"No-o," Malcolm said, shaking his head. "It still wouldn't — it —"

"I've simply got to talk to Mrs. Coverlet," declared Mr. Romaine. "Obviously there's some misunderstanding. She's probably angry at me for not getting over to your place to see her. But I've tried to call her a dozen times at least, and she's never in. She doesn't even phone me back!"

"I'm afraid she'll be out all day today, too, sir," Molly informed the grocer.

Mr. Romaine opened his mouth to say something but changed his mind. Instead, he looked rather sharply at the children, with an expression which reminded Molly unpleasantly of the way Miss Eva had regarded them over the handle of her lawn mower the other day.

Malcolm thought it advisable to change the subject. "Uh, Mr. Romaine," he said, "about the turtle meat —"

"Turtle meat? Oh, yes," the grocer answered vaguely. "The waste cans are in the back room — you remember."

When the children came back a few minutes later with

a lovely chunk of smelly stew meat, such as turtles love, carefully wrapped in newspaper, Mr. Romaine was still standing just as they had left him, with a perplexed look on his red face, drumming his fingers on the counter.

"Thanks a lot, Mr. Romaine!" they called politely as they left. But Mr. Romaine, biting his lip, and twiddling his fingers, said nothing at all, and did not even seem to notice them go.

If you've ever been turtling in a slough, you know that the way to do it is to tie a piece of nicely rotten meat to a string. Then you lower it into the water and wait. People who have small flat-bottomed boats are lucky, of course, because they can get out into the middle of things. But for those without — like the Persevers, for instance — nearly every slough has logs or rocks or trees with leaning branches which serve very well as places to sit. After you have found a good spot for yourself — unfortunately, there are always a few choice places which everybody re-members from last time and wants, and therefore some un-avoidable arguments — after you have gotten settled to wait for your turtle, there is nothing pleasanter in the world than to watch the things that go on in a slough. The most interesting cans and bottles are apt to be bobbing, half drowned, all about you; and sometimes, if you're lucky, one will give a gulp and sink before your eyes. Bold gangs of ducks come past and stare and talk about you to your face in such a ridiculously rude way that you have to laugh. As a rule, you can't see the bottom of a slough because the water is so thick and green. But, as if to make up for this, the surface of a slough is usually more beautifully decorated with floating moss and water lilies than any other kind of water.

Out in the middle of the slough near the Persevers' house there was the body of an old car. How it ever got there, they used to wonder and ponder. In late summer — as it was that August day — the water was very low, and you could see most of the car, even the top of its wheels, and it looked like just what it was — a funny old wreck, the color of rust. But in the spring, when the water was high, only its hollow headlights and the snout of its hood stuck out, and then the Persevers pretended the slough was an African water hole, and the car a hippopotamus rising from his mud bath.

There were thousands and thousands of insects in the air above the Persevers' slough, mainly the everyday nuisances — flies and mosquitoes. But in the slough itself were wonderful water bugs with their black oars and sharp beaks. And there were brown-black leeches, tirelessly stretching and squeezing themselves small, like springs; and now and then a seagoing snake, using his narrow tail for a rudder. I know that many people prefer to go to lakes and ocean

110

beaches for water sports; yet the Persever children were content with their slough and thought it the most interesting place in the world.

Sooner or later, as each one waited in his special niche, somebody would feel a turtle grab at his bait. The minute this happened, he gave a sharp whistle for the net man, and then slowly, smoothly, without a single jerk to frighten the turtle, he would draw the string to the surface. Meanwhile he could hear the net man plunging and stumbling toward him along the bank, through mud and underbrush and stiff ferns. Handling the net was the choicest job of all. The three children were supposed to take turns being net man, but for some reason it was always Malcolm's turn. When Molly and the Toad remarked about this, Malcolm looked hurt and explained that handling the net was such a dangerously tricky job that it was really too much for the younger ones to try.

When the string had been pulled out of the water just far enough so that you could make out the turtle, the net man, in one skillful movement, scooped his net down into and out of the water again, bringing up the amazed little animal. Naturally, you wouldn't expect that such a difficult operation could be done successfully every time! What frequently happened was that the net man would lean over just an inch too far, lose his balance, and while slipping and struggling on the log or rock, take hold of the person

with the turtle on the string, and then they would both fall in. But the water wasn't deep, scarcely up to their hips any place, and pleasantly cool, and why do you think they were wearing their slough clothes, anyway?

In spite of its being such a difficult sport, the Persevers usually succeeded in capturing at least one turtle. Then all three of them would gather on the bank to see if it was a snapper. They had never actually caught a snapping turtle, but this did not discourage them. Somebody always held out a twig to see if he would bite it in two, but so far all the turtles had only blinked their dry eyelids at the stick and turned their heads away.

Whenever one of the Persevers caught a turtle, there was a little rash talk about making turtle soup, but it never came to any more than talk. And after they had squatted beside him for a while, turning him over and admiring the designs on his stomach, and comparing him to other interesting turtles in the past, they would set him right side up again and watch him scuttle down the bank and plop into the slough.

At the end of this latest, beautiful day at the slough, the Persevers were making their way back home. Their faces were stiff with streaks of mud and stinging from sunburn. Their sneakers squished, and their damp blue jeans gave off the rich and curious smell of the black mud from the bottom. They were perfectly happy, and as they came around the corner into their own street, the Toad was lustily singing, "Ah — I come from Alabama with a Band-Aid on my knee."

Molly had just murmured, "Banjo, Toad!" in a friendly way when Malcolm, who was a few steps ahead of them, stopped abruptly. Then the two younger ones, coming up behind him, saw a blue delivery truck in front of their house. Inside it were cartons with cereal boxes, ginger ale bottles, and carrot greens sticking over their tops.

"Mr. Romaine!" the Toad whispered, peering around Malcolm's arm. "Quick, let's go back to the slough!"

"It's no use. We'll have to face him," said Malcolm bravely. "Maybe it won't be too bad."

But they had not gone many steps farther when even Malcolm gave up trying to look cheerful, for glancing up at their house, they saw, looking down at them from the front window, Mr. Forthright, Mr. Romaine, and Miss Eva Penalty.

Mr. Romaine looked red and bewildered. Miss Eva's eyes were blinking as rapidly as bats' wings, and she looked hungrily and joyfully at the Toad. Mr. Forthright was gazing straight into Malcolm's eyes, pale and reproachful.

Chapter XVI

"MRS. COVERLET'S been away since when?" Mr. Forthright asked incredulously.

"Since June," Malcolm told him with a gulp. In the middle of the living room stood the three Persever children, close together in one unhappily squirming lump. Miss Eva, Mr. Romaine, and Mr. Forthright sat in a stiff row on the living-room couch looking at them.

"But if she was in Duluth, how could she make the Heather's Temptation?" asked Mr. Romaine in confusion.

"She didn't," Molly told him for the third time. "The Toad invented it for a tonic for his cat." The children had been explaining and explaining about Mrs. Coverlet, and selling Nervous, and making Heather's Temptation, ever since they had gotten back from the slough, and still none of the grownups seemed able to take it in.

"Only we ran out of vitamins," finished the Toad, "or else nobody would ever have found out."

"Oh, I was suspicious, all right," Miss Eva declared proudly. "And when I saw Mr. Romaine knocking and knocking at the door today, I finally came over. I said, 'Mr. Romaine, if you ask *me*, there's something funny going on here, and *I* think it's time we called Mr. Forthright!' "

"But why did you want to keep it a secret about Mrs. Coverlet's being away, in the first place?" Mr. Forthright wanted to know. And here, all Malcolm could do was look pleadingly and silently at his friend, as if begging him to understand that there were things impossible to explain before certain people.

Mr. Romaine, looking exhausted and depressed, rose heavily to his feet. "I'll be running along," he said. "Still have orders to deliver before supper." On his way out he passed Heather, sitting in a patch of sun on the porch, washing her white fur sandals with her useful pink tongue. "Cat food!" Mr. Romaine muttered. "How could *I* know it was cat food?" Heather paid no attention to him.

Miss Eva, unfortunately, showed no signs of leaving. She looked as cheerful and alert as a cat watching a mouse hole, and perfectly willing to wait there all day. At last Mr. Forthright said, "Forgive me, Miss Eva, but there are some personal things — I wonder — "

"Why, of course, Reverend!" Miss Eva exclaimed, bouncing off the sofa with a bright smile. "I've got to be getting home, anyway, to air the guest room and make up the bed for Theobold. I'm going to put a little barley gruel on the stove for his supper, too. Heaven only knows what he's been eating these last months!" As she passed the small, scowling Toad, her nose caught a whiff of slough from his pants. "And a good hot bath with plenty of green soap!" they heard her say rapturously, rubbing her hands in anticipation as she hurried away.

When she had gone, Malcolm cleared his throat. "The reason we didn't tell anybody Mrs. Coverlet was gone," he blurted, "was that we wanted to stay here together, sir! The Toad just would *not* go to Miss Eva's!"

Mr. Forthright looked at the Toad in surprise. The Toad, I am sorry to say, only glared back at him impolitely, wiggling his muddy toes irritably up and down in the large holes in the fronts of his sneakers. "But, Toad," the minister told him kindly, "Miss Eva is awfully fond of you. She spoke to your father before he left and they agreed that if any emergency came up, you were to go to her house, and I would sleep up here to keep an eye on the bigger ones!"

"All *I* know is —" growled the shocking little boy. "All *I* know is that if I have to go to Miss Eva's, then I'm sorry I ever said my prayers at night!" Here Malcolm and Molly gaped at their little brother in horror, but the Toad went on regardless, eying Mr. Forthright bitterly all the while, as if the Toad held him personally accountable for what had happened. "Every night since Mrs. Coverlet went, I've said, 'Lead us not into temptation and deliver me from Eva,' " he told the minister, "and it didn't do any good at all!"

Mr. Forthright opened his mouth at once to say something to the Toad but apparently decided it would be quite useless. Instead, he turned to Molly. "Go help the Toad clean up a bit, Molly dear, and put his things in a suitcase. Miss Eva will be waiting."

When they were alone, Mr. Forthright said to Malcolm, "I'm sorry the Toad feels this way. Miss Eva is a far kinder person than you children give her credit for. It's too bad you've never made an effort to know her better." He looked at Malcolm for a long moment. "How did you think this would end, Malcolm? You must have known somebody would find out!"

"For one thing, we didn't realize Mrs. Coverlet would be gone so long," Malcolm admitted. "And then, as the summer went on, we got so busy making money, we didn't have time to worry."

A new shadow crossed Mr. Forthright's face. "Didn't you ever write your father about money, Malcolm? After your promise to me that night?"

"Oh, I wrote him all right." Here Malcolm looked away. "Only not about money."

Mr. Forthright turned his eyes sorrowfully to the floor.

"But we didn't need to write him! We made lots and lots of it ourselves! We were just about ready to send Dad some!"

Still Mr. Forthright did not answer or look up, and Malcolm knew how deeply his behavior had stung his good friend. It seemed to him that since it was his fault that Mr. Forthright felt so badly, the least he could do was think of something to say to cheer him. He felt pretty sure that the minister would feel better if he were to assure him that he saw now how wrong they had been, and that he was terribly sorry about everything. And several times Malcolm actually took a big breath and opened his mouth to say these things. But then he would suddenly think about the summer — how he and Molly and the Toad had stayed together and helped each other, and managed beautifully all by themselves; how hard and how profitably they had worked; how much less than usual they had argued and scrapped (they hadn't had time); and how they had not worried their father, but had helped him instead — and poor honest Malcolm found in his heart that he did not regret what they had done and could not tell Mr. Forthright that he was sorry. He could only look miserably at his friend and think what a trying thing it was to have been born with such a complicated conscience.

All at once, to both his and Mr. Forthright's relief, the

telephone in the hall began to ring. Malcolm started to go to it, but Mr. Forthright was closer and picked it up himself. When he came back into the living room a minute later, he was looking happier than he had all afternoon. "A telegram from Duluth!" he said. "Mrs. Coverlet gets back on Friday!"

"Who was on the phone?" curious Molly called from the head of the stairs.

"A telegram from Mrs. Coverlet!" Malcolm answered her joyfully. "She's coming home!"

"Great!" yelled the Toad as he jumped down the front stairs two at a time. "Now I don't have to go to Miss Eva's, and I can get these awful, uncomfortable clothes off again!" He was wearing a clean white shirt and starched pants, and he smelled abnormally of soap.

"I'm afraid you'll still have to go, Toad," Mr. Forthright told him. "Today's only Monday, but everything will be back to normal on Friday, thank heavens!"

"I'll bring down your suitcase, Toady!" Molly called down sadly.

"We'll see you every day, you know," added Malcolm.

They were standing in the vestibule in a dejected little group, waiting for Molly to come down with the suitcase, when the front doorbell rang, and everybody jumped. When Malcolm opened the door, a man in black uniform with a shiny patent-leather visor on his cap was standing there.

"Good afternoon," he said. "Is Master Theobold ready? Oh, yes, I can see that he is!" He was looking at the Toad in his best clothes, and at Molly coming down the stairs with a suitcase in her hand. Doffing his black cap, he stepped inside the Persevers' vestibule and took the bag from Molly.

"I beg your pardon," said Mr. Forthright, looking bewildered, "but who —"

"I am Wheeler, sir, from Mrs. Dextrose-Chesapeake. She wrote some weeks ago, I believe, to ask Master Theobold to visit her in New York at this time. And she sent me to bring him today, as arranged. I'm sure I was expected, wasn't I?" he asked, looking inquiringly at the three children.

"We did get a letter!" Malcolm exclaimed, suddenly remembering.

"But, my goodness! Is today the twenty-seventh already?" asked Molly, mortified to have forgotten.

"So much has been happening that we —"

"Who cares! Who cares!" the Toad cried joyously. He grabbed the chauffeur's free hand and began to pull him toward the front door with all his might and main. "I'm ready! Let's *go!*"

"Now, wait, Theobold!" Mr. Forthright said sternly. "I'm entirely confused. Who is Mrs. Dextrose-Chesapeake, and why are you going to New York?"

"It's the cat lady who bought Nervous," Malcolm explained.

"Oh, please let him go, Mr. Forthright!" Molly begged, putting her hand on the minister's arm.

"You can call Dr. Furry and ask him about her if you don't believe us," Malcolm said humbly. "But she's awfully nice, and the Toad likes her!"

"He's going to get to see Nervous in a cat show and go to museums and zoos and everything. Oh, *let* him go, Mr. Forthright!" Molly pleaded.

"When would he come home?" Mr. Forthright asked Wheeler, the chauffeur. "That is, if I *do* let him —"

"The same day Mrs. Coverlet gets back," interrupted the Toad. "When is that, anyway? Oh, yes, Friday! I'll be back Friday!"

Mr. Forthright looked doubtfully from the Toad, who was frantically yanking at the chauffeur's sleeve, to the Toad's older brother and sister, who were looking up at him anxiously. Malcolm and Molly did not know it, of course, but they had never looked nicer to Mr. Forthright than they did at that moment, with their tired, muddy faces, pleading for their little brother. Mr. Forthright thought to himself that really, in spite of the extraordinary — and, you might even say, dishonest — way they had spent the summer, he liked the Persevers better than any children he knew.

"Go along, then, Toad!" said the minister at last. "And have a good time in New York!"

The Toad ran in circles of excitement around Wheeler as the two of them went down the front walk to Mrs. Dextrose-Chesapeake's car. "G'by, you guys!" he called back. "Don't forget to feed all my cats! I hid some extra Heathther's Temptation behind the radiator in the bathroom so they'd have plenty. G'by!" They watched him jump into the front seat beside Wheeler and drive away triumphantly.

Mr. Forthright laid a friendly arm over Malcolm's and Molly's shoulders. " 'Deliver me from Eva,' " he said under his breath. "It looks as if the Toad's prayer was answered, after all. I'll have to remind him of that when he gets back.

"By the way," he remarked as the three of them stood looking down at the empty street, where the green afternoon shadows had gathered, "I have a feeling it must be getting on toward supper. Somebody left a lovely cold barbecued chicken on my back porch this afternoon. And there's most of a blueberry pie in my pantry, and a loaf of cinnamon bread we could toast. Why don't we all go on down to my house? I have to go back sometime this evening, anyway, to get my pajamas, so I can stay with you."

Malcolm and Molly gave two tremendous heartfelt sighs. They were really awfully tired, they suddenly realized, and Mr. Forthright's supper sounded too good to be true after all those weeks of hamburgers and chocolate ice cream.

"Oh, but, Mr. Forthright," said practical Molly as they started down the walk, "what about Miss Eva? I mean — hadn't we better tell her about the Toad so she can take the barley gruel off the stove and all?"

"Oh, Lord!" murmured Mr. Forthright, while a faint frown passed over his kind face. Immediately he looked sorry he had said it. "Thank you for reminding me, Molly," he told her politely. "But why don't we call her on the phone from my house? It'll be easier that way, don't you think?"

"Much easier!" agreed Malcolm and Molly as they looked across the grass and beyond the chestnut tree at Miss Eva's prim white house. "Much easier!" they said again as they hurried along toward Mr. Forthright's good, cold supper.

Chapter XVII

AFTER that, things suddenly became amazingly peaceful for Malcolm and Molly. Of course, the Toad was away and that in itself was restful. Also, Mr. Forthright came up and spent the nights at their house, and they found it comfortable having him around. Malcolm and Molly had forgotten how pleasant it was to have a grownup in the house at night. They had never mentioned it to each other, of course, but it had always seemed a little lonely that summer to turn off all the lights themselves at bedtime and leave the downstairs behind them empty and dark. After a few days Malcolm's old grass customers began to call him about resuming work on their lawns, for the supply of Heather's Temptation was quickly dwindling in the neighborhood. Speaking of Heather's Temptation, the children found a large quantity of it behind the bathroom radiator. The Toad had

125

made certain that Heather and her kittens had at least a year's supply.

Then on Thursday morning a cable arrived from New Zealand. It said:

ARRIVING SATURDAY, SEPTEMBER 1. MINE OPERATING WELL. HAVE A GOOD MANAGER. SUCCESSFUL SUMMER. LOVE. DAD

"Thank heaven!" breathed Mr. Forthright.

On Friday, the last day of August, Mrs. Coverlet got back from Duluth. When she heard all that had happened during her absence, the poor soul sat down on a kitchen chair and wept. "I may as well leave me things packed," she sobbed. "Your dear father will cast me out in the street when he hears."

Mr. Forthright promised her that nothing of the sort would happen. At this, Mrs. Coverlet brightened enough to look around, admire Heather and the kittens, whom she had never seen, and listen in amazement to the story of how funny-looking old Nervous had turned out to be handsome, famous, and valuable. Then she went to her room, took off her best hat, put on her working clothes, and began to clean the house. Molly was just a little annoyed that Mrs. Coverlet should think there was so much to be done

126

in that direction. It seemed to her that they had kept the house very tidy indeed. But Mrs. Coverlet, going from room to room clicking her tongue, merely said that she wished it were a week from Saturday and not tomorrow that Mr. Persever was getting home.

At four o'clock Friday afternoon the Toad returned triumphantly from New York. "Well, I'm back," he shouted from the front door, as if now that *he* was there, they could all begin to live again. He was a little stouter and a great deal cockier than before, and the first thing Mrs. Coverlet did was to kneel down and hug and kiss him. The Toad was in such good spirits that in spite of the fact that he hated this sort of thing, he kindly stood still and let Mrs. Coverlet do it, as a special treat for her. Even Molly and Malcolm had to admit that they were glad to see him again. For some reason you couldn't help being fond of the Toad, particularly when you had been working at civilizing him as long and as hard as they had.

The next afternoon, Malcolm, Molly, and the Toad were sitting under the chestnut tree in their back yard. Reverend Forthright had gone alone to meet their father at the airport. "I know you'd like to go with me," he had told them, "but I have to break some things to your father about the summer — I'm sure you three know what I mean. And I think it might be better if I saw him first and got it over with." All things considered, the children were inclined

to agree with Mr. Forthright; and so there they sat, under the tree, a little quieter than usual, watching Heather give her kittens their first lesson in tree climbing. Whenever one of the little cats got up as high as the first branch of the chestnut, which Heather thought was plenty far, she would give the Toad an anxious look, and he would reach up and pry the little thing gently from the bark and set it on the grass again.

Through the open doors and windows of their house they could hear the sound of upheaval within. Sometimes it was the growl of furniture being pulled out from the wall; sometimes it was the pitiful squeal of a window being scrubbed; and among all these sounds, the vacuum cleaner roared and whined without stopping. Since early morning Mrs. Coverlet and her friend Miss Eva Penalty had been hard at work. A wide-awake smell of bleach and furniture polish came out of doors and bothered the lazy do-nothing air in the Persevers' late summer garden.

"Maybe Dad won't be *too* mad," Malcolm remarked, leaning his back against the trunk of the chestnut tree and chewing a blade of grass.

"It's just a shame he didn't need the money we made," muttered Molly. "The cablegram said the mine is a great success."

Suddenly the two older Persevers turned and frowned at their little brother, who had been lying on his back nearby and now for some reason had begun to giggle foolishly. Then they saw that the white kitten had put both paws around his neck and was earnestly licking his ear. When he saw them both watching him disapprovingly, the Toad sat up. "Hey, you should see Nervous!" he told them. "He's the richest and famousest cat in the world!" All the Toad wanted to talk about since getting home was Nervous and New York.

"I'm sure there are lots of famous cats besides Nervous," Molly said severely.

"Richest and famousest cat in the world," repeated the Toad, "but of course he knows *me!* I'm going to visit Mrs. Dextrose-Chesapeake again in Christmas vacation," he went on. "She's *neat*. She has the biggest house in the world, and it has an elevator in it. She lets *me* run it, of course. Boy, you guys would really like New York! Do you want me to ask Mrs. Dextrose-Chesapeake if you can come, too?" At this he gave his brother and sister a superior and generous smile.

Molly and Malcolm stared grimly at the Toad. He really had been unbearable since getting home. *He* wasn't worried about what their father would have to say about their highly unusual summer! He was much too pleased with himself to have a care in the world. When they thought of all they had been through to keep him out of Miss Eva's clutches this summer, and how unconcerned and

130

ungrateful the Toad seemed, they really wondered if it had been worth it.

At that very minute Miss Eva herself, wearing a dust turban around her head and an apron over her dress, came down the back steps of their house and across the lawn toward them. "We're just about through in there," she said, pulling off a pair of rubber work gloves, "so I'll be getting home." Suddenly she frowned. "Now, listen, children," she told them, flickering her eyes behind her glasses, "I wish to know the instant your father gets back! I want to tell him the whole story of what happened here this summer." The children, who had gotten politely to their feet when she came over to them and were all holding various cats in their arms, glanced uneasily at each other. Wouldn't it be horrible if after Mr. Forthright had explained everything to their father in the nicest possible way, Miss Eva were to give him a black picture of the summer the minute he got home!

"I want to tell him," Miss Eva said, "that he is not to be angry with any of you! You didn't mean any harm, and you're not bad children — just a little too imaginative and undisciplined." Her fluttery gaze fell upon the Toad, who, with his eyes tightly squeezed shut in order not to have to look at Miss Eva, was quickly rubbing his nose against Heather's beautiful lavender back. "Only, when I think of poor little Theobold," she said softly, "alone all summer,

131

with no one to look after him, or tuck him in and kiss him good night" — here the Toad shivered violently — "while I had so much time on my hands and that empty house —" Here Miss Eva broke off and hurried away across the yard to her home. Malcolm and Molly stared after her.

"She's really not so bad, you know!" murmured Molly, looking very surprised.

"Thanks, Miss Eva!" Malcolm called after her. "We'll let you know as soon as Dad gets here!" Malcolm now frowned meaningfully at his little brother, who was once more stretched out comfortably on the grass among his many cats. "*Some* people I could mention ought to try to be more polite to Miss Eva," he said sternly, and then added softly, "Mr. Forthright is right. None of us has ever really tried to be friends with her."

"Heck!" said the Toad, sticking out his lower lip. "We had a lot more fun being on our own. This is the best summer we've ever had, and you know it!"

"We did do pretty well," Malcolm had to agree, lowering himself down on the grass once more.

"If only Dad understands," sighed Molly.

All at once they heard Mr. Forthright's old car come to a wheezing stop in front of their house. Its door slammed. "Where are these guilty rascals?" came their father's great voice, deeper and more booming than they ever remembered. The children looked at each other with big eyes.

"Isn't anybody home?" he called again. Then Mr. Forth-right's voice said something, and all of a sudden they heard their father's familiar laugh, cheerful and full of enthusiasm, and perfectly good-humored.

"I don't think he's really mad at all," whispered Malcolm, and the sad corners of his mouth twitched up. Suddenly all three children jumped to their feet, spilling the six insulted cats from their laps, and ran pell-mell around the house and down the path to meet him.